A
Rainbow
of
Spells

© Studio Republic

About the Author

Ileana Abrev (Queensland, Australia) has been a practicing witch for more than twenty years. With knowledge passed down to her by her father, an esteemed Santero, Ileana guides her clients on a daily basis to solve problems while assisting them with spell casting for a positive outcome. She is the author of *The Little Big Book of White Spells*, *Mindful Mama*, and *A Rainbow of Spells*.

A Rainbow of Spells

Manifesting with Color

Ileana Abrev

LLEWELLYN PUBLICATIONS | WOODBURY, MINNESOTA

First Edition
First Printing, 2023

Book design by Samantha Peterson
Cover art by Saskia Bueno
Cover design by Kevin R. Brown
Interior art by Llewellyn Art Department

Llewellyn Publications is a registered trademark of Llewellyn Worldwide Ltd.

Library of Congress Cataloging-in-Publication Data (Pending)
ISBN: 978-0-7387-7226-4

Llewellyn Worldwide Ltd. does not participate in, endorse, or have any authority or responsibility concerning private business transactions between our authors and the public.

All mail addressed to the author is forwarded but the publisher cannot, unless specifically instructed by the author, give out an address or phone number.

Any internet references contained in this work are current at publication time, but the publisher cannot guarantee that a specific location will continue to be maintained. Please refer to the publisher's website for links to authors' websites and other sources.

Llewellyn Publications
A Division of Llewellyn Worldwide Ltd.
2143 Wooddale Drive
Woodbury, MN 55125-2989
www.llewellyn.com

Printed in China

Other Books by Ileana Abrev

The Little Big Book of White Spells

Mindful Mama

To Clara and Emmett, you are the colors in my world.
To Elysia, a heartfelt thank you for the last ten and
a half years and for being behind my every email.

Contents

Part II: Color Magic in Everyday Life

Disclaimer

The information provided in this book is not a substitution for consulting a medical health care professional. All the information in this book, including the information related to mental health, physical health, medical conditions, crystals, and treatments, is for educational, informational, and entertainment purposes only. Please consult a health care professional before starting any crystal or essential oil treatments. For diagnosis or treatment of any medical condition, readers are advised to seek the services of a competent medical professional.

While best efforts have been used in preparing this book, neither the author nor the publisher shall be held liable or responsible to any person or entity with respect to any loss or damages caused, or alleged to have been caused, directly or indirectly, by the information contained herein. Every situation is different, and the advice and strategies contained in this book may not be suitable for your situation.

In the following pages you will find recommendations for the use of certain herbs, essential oils, and blends. If you are allergic to any of these items, please refrain from use. Do your own research before using an essential oil. Each body reacts differently to herbs, essential oils, and other items, so results may vary person to person. Essential oils are potent; use care when handling them. Always dilute essential oils before placing them on your skin, and make sure to do a patch test on your skin before use. Never ingest essential oils. Some herbal remedies can react with prescription or over-the-counter medications in adverse ways. If you are on medication or have health issues, please do not ingest any herbs without first consulting a qualified practitioner.

Some crystals are toxic, harmful, or poisonous if left on the skin. Other crystals are toxic, harmful, or poisonous if ingested in any way. Always do your research before handling a crystal, especially if you have never worked with that specific crystal before. If you are allergic to any of the crystals suggested in this book, please refrain from use. When making crystal-infused water, be extremely cautious, do your research, and make sure the crystal is nontoxic before ingesting any crystal-infused water. Never ingest a crystal.

Introduction

Magic has been a part of my life for decades now. I was born into it. My father was a spiritual medium and, later in life, a santero. A *santero* is a priest in the religious beliefs of Santeria, a practice brought to Cuba by the Yoruba tribe from Nigeria. The Yoruba people were able to identify their own deities with the Catholic saints and in turn gave them the names according to their own deities' strengths and beliefs. This became a religious practice known as Lucumi, which is still practiced in Cuba and around the world to this day.

Even though I loved Santeria, later in life I turned to witchcraft, which doesn't have the mystery and the secrecy that Santeria has. It was refreshing to work with nature and its essence without engaging in retaliation, which Santeria taps into (depending on the santero) from time to time. During my time with Santeria, I learned about its origins and practices. I sometimes use it in conjunction with my witchcraft, especially when using color to cause a needed effect.

I have been a solitary witch for decades now, writing, practicing, and recommending spells for those needing a change in life. Spell-work helps people find their way when they feel lost, heal relationships that have become stagnant over time, improve financial matters, protect loved ones from negative energies, find love within, manifest romantic love, and everything in between.

The good thing about this book is you don't have to be a witch to utilize the power of a spell. You don't even have to be a magical practitioner! Anyone can tap into magical forces—there is no contract or entry fee. Magic is a free membership of unlimited access to self-improvement. It provides potential much greater than you've ever known, and once the doors open, the possibilities are endless. Magic uses our desires and/or daily rites of passage to upgrade, enhance, and enrich our lives whenever possible. Magic can also help us accept or work through things that are troubling us. The only thing we need to start making magic is a spell. And your spell carries no matter if you are a witch or not.

Spells work because they tap into Mother Nature's natural resources. Mother Nature's natural resources are just about everything we can see, touch, or smell. There is always a color associated with natural resources, whether they are flowers, herbs, crystals, trees, oceans, or even mountains. Everything around us can be identified by its color and essence. All natural resources enhance our spiritual awareness of the world we live in. When we use Mother Nature's resources as needed, we better ourselves in every way imaginable during the process.

Another aspect of spellwork is working with the universal forces we can't see (as well as those we *can* see) in our solar system, like the planets and stars. Each one resonates with a particular color, and seven of them align with a particular day of the week. Yes, these massive, faraway universal forces have an influence on our spellwork!

For example, let's say you want to do a love spell. The first thing you need to do is identify the color associated with love, and then identify the planetary force that manifests love. The color would be pink or red, and the planet would be Venus. Once you have identified these pieces, you can start to build your spell using the necessary tools: Mother Nature's natural resources. You could use candles, crystals, flowers, herbs, and other objects that resonate within those forces to create magic.

A key component of all magic is color. You could even say color is an accessory that magic cannot do without. I love the way color is a part of every spell, particularly when it comes to candle magic. In this book, I will show you that you can blend color into your spells to manifest your deepest desires and banish your worries.

This book contains dozens of spells, some lengthy and others simple and straight to the point. Each spell in this book uses at least one color that corresponds to a magical intent. This book is inspired by the rainbow, so it begins with the first color of the rainbow, red. The following chapters are in the same order as the colors of the rainbow. I've also included several chapters for colors that are not part of the rainbow, because other colors on the spectrum are just as powerful.

As you make your way through this book, you will learn which color(s), day of the week, and planet correspond with your spellwork. But before we can dive into spellwork, we have to create a sacred space for our magic. Chapter 1 of this book discusses how to create your very own sacred space for your magical workings.

Before we begin, though, I want to talk a little bit more about magic. I believe magic surrounds our daily lives and affirms its existence whenever we are in awe of a beautiful sunrise or sunset, a captivating moon, a seedling, a bird chirping, a pregnant woman, a child learning to walk, an elderly couple holding hands, a bouquet of flowers, a happy ending, an amazing rainbow, or the beauty of nature. We harvest nature's energy daily, even if it is just to water our garden. All in all, magic is the planet we inhabit in all its glory.

When we practice magic, we are tapping into the precious gifts bestowed upon us that we often take for granted. We can reach out and harvest the energy nature provides and manipulate it for our own needs. Nature's resources are amply available at any time of the day, morning, noon, and night. Another resource we always have available to us are our guardian angels and spiritual guides. A lot of the time, we are not aware of their presence, but from time to time they appear in our lives offering guidance, love, and acceptance, often in the form of a friend or a dream.

Never underestimate the power we can tap into, but always do it with caution and for the benefit of all. Understanding the balance of positive and negative magic is key to successful magical workings that have a positive effect.

People put strong emphasis on the positive and negative sides of magic. We all have the power to do both—it is how we wish to practice magic that makes it positive or negative. Usually, people who are motivated by vengeance and jealousy can only inflict negative magic, as they are wishing someone harm. Additionally, if your magic is motivated by greed, it is not positive magic. However, those of us who practice a positive lifestyle can only practice what is known as positive magic.

There are many ways you can practice magic without being negative. If you want someone to leave you alone, don't light black candles and wish them harm; light a black and a white candle and wish them on their merry way. This is just one example of how to work positively for the good of all. It is always possible to protect and defend ourselves without being vicious or harmful to others. When a spell is conducted in a negative manner to cause harm, manipulate, or change another's destiny, you are asking for trouble, and you're playing with Karma.

Karma is the law of the Universe, the justice system that keeps the balance of good and evil. All who are true practitioners believe and respect the oath "Harm none, for if you do, it will come back to you in three."

Black or white, positive or negative, yin or yang, you must be able to understand both, to be in tune with the forces of nature and the Universe. Search your heart, look deep into your soul, and find your true side so that you do not disturb the balance between you and nature. Above all, never inflict your will on others. And if you still haven't worked out which side you fall on, consider the following: "If you don't like someone doing it to you, don't do it to them."

Connecting positive thoughts to nature's resources allows us to send a message to the Universe to cause an effect. If you believe in your actions, yourself, and the Universe, your needs will manifest in front of your eyes. When they do, you have created positive magic. Think of magic as a never-ending power source you can plug into any time. Knowing this, why wouldn't you take advantage of what is freely available in the form of a spell?

A spell is the art of sharing your needs with the Universe using words or chants to summon universal forces or spirits to aid you with your endeavor. A spell does not have to be complex, but it's also not as simple as saying "Abracadabra!" In every spell there is a sense of hope for a contented future filled with love, health, and happiness. Sometimes, even if our lives are all mapped out, we occasionally take a wrong turn, and when we do, turning to magical measures can help us get back on track.

At one time, magic was very much tolerated and practiced freely. Unfortunately, over the centuries, the art of spellcasting took a few steps backward and became practiced sparingly. These days, spellwork is typically done only after a dire situation arises—a situation that might have been avoided if a spell had been done in the first place. Most of us seek magic when everything else we've tried has failed; we ask the cosmos for help, hoping it can fix the situation we've found ourselves in (or at least lessen the impact).

What's great about magic is that it doesn't matter if you reach out to the cosmos at the beginning, middle, or end of a situation; the only thing that matters is that you reached out. The exciting thing about spellwork is that you already know what you want to manifest, and just thinking about it makes your intent known to universal forces, and they start listening.

One thing I love about spellwork is that it is fun to put spells together. When blending energies, you need to make sure you have the right tools for your spell. This can be accomplished relatively easily with correlation, the proper tools, and projection.

Correlation: Summoning universal forces, the planets, the days of the week, and/or colors that correspond with your intent.

Gathering the Tools: Figuring out what is needed for the spell, such as which herbs, colors, candles, or crystals to use. As you gather the tools for your spell, you will subconsciously start focusing and concentrating on your intent.

Projection: This is when you project your needs out to the cosmos with conviction, passion, and purpose.

Please join me as I guide you on this extraordinary, wonderful journey of connecting spells with color in a fun and easy way. You are ready to make your desires known to the Universe, and all you need are positive thoughts, corresponding colors, and some magical tools.

1
Creating Your Sacred Space

If you already have a sacred space, that's great; you know how important it is to have a place to conduct your magical workings. A sacred space is the place where you keep your magical tools, and it's also home to all your candleholders.

Creating your sacred space is the perfect way to start this book; it's the beginning of your journey and a great introduction to magic. It will also be a major focal point when you do your spells. Your sacred space will need to be a place where you feel comfortable and at peace, and it also needs to be somewhere you will not be disturbed.

Your sacred space and what you do there will end up being a tremendous part of your magic. Keep in mind, you have total control of what you do in your sacred space. There is no need to tell anyone about it if you don't wish to do so; it can be a totally private space. Your sacred space could be a room in your home, a small office space, a room that is rarely used, or even a shed or porch area that is not being used. If you don't have much space, you could set up your sacred space in a closet or on a windowsill. You could also make your sacred space mobile so that you can pack it up when it is not needed; for this, I'd recommend using an object like a chest, something that has a lid, so that once you open it, you know you are ready to do magic. Some people set up sacred space in their living area or bedroom. Personally, I do not want anyone in the same room as me unless I am doing a spiritual cleansing for someone. Think about what sort of sacred space suits you best. You are in total control of this space, and you always will be. As I said before, it will become a focal point of your magical life and end up being a part of you.

The more you work in your sacred space, the more comfortable it will become. You may add or remove items from your sacred space as you settle in. Eventually, you will start to feel at home in your sacred space. Once you truly believe your sacred space is the heart of your magical practice, you have made a connection with the Universe. Through this connection, you have bound your sacred space with the magical essence of all that is out there for the taking, such as the elements, the planets, and even the lunar phases.

With time, you will feel so comfortable in this sacred space that you may not be able to work magic anywhere else. It's not uncommon for your sacred space to become a respite for you even when you're not doing spellwork; perhaps you will spend time there when you want to meditate, journal, or simply find peace of mind.

If you already have a sacred space, you may already have the tools needed to do spellwork, but for those of you who are new to this (or just want to refresh your space), the rest of this chapter will discuss items you may want to incorporate into your sacred space. The following list is a good starting point, but of course I cannot mention everything. Decorate your sacred space in the way that feels right to you. Find items at your local magical supply store or the nearest botanica. You can even shop online and have everything at your fingertips.

Preparing Your Sacred Space

Keep this in mind as you start to think about what is needed for your sacred space: you have already started this magical and spiritual chapter of your life. Above all, have fun, and always try to maintain a positive outlook about the outcome. If you keep your heart and soul open to limitless possibilities, you'll be rewarded when you least expect it.

Okay, let's get started!

Table

Your sacred space will need a table or something similar. The item you choose can be any height as long as it is a flat surface. You may want to use an old dresser and stash your tools in the drawers. A coffee table works well, as you can sit on floor cushions to meditate and work on your visualization. Let us call this the foundation of your sacred space.

Table Covering

You will need to cover your table to keep the surface protected. A plain purple tablecloth is ideal, though the fabric you choose does not matter. You could even use a purple scarf with different tones of purples, mauves, or violets; these colors look impressive together. The most important thing is that the base color of your table covering is purple.

This ancient color was once used only by those with wealth, power, and status. Purple was known as the color of kings, as the dye was too expensive for the common people to afford. Therefore, it became the color of power and strength. This makes it the perfect color for your sacred space.

Candleholders

You are going to need a few candleholders, not only for your spells but for ambience as well. I recommend having tapered, votive, and tealight candleholders. Some people like glass candleholders, while others prefer brass, ceramic, or wooden. Remember, the more satisfied you are with the items you choose, the better you'll feel when doing spells. It is like wearing an old dress you've always disliked to a party: you still looked good, but you would have felt better if you'd bought a new one for the occasion.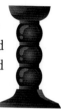

Your candleholders should reflect your taste and what you are attracted to. (Bonus points if you can find purple ones! Then you are ready for communication with the Universe.) Think about using your sacred space as a marketing tool: the more attractive the presentation is, the more business you attract—except, in this case, you are attracting universal forces, not people. Universal forces are not looking for a perfect display, but rather the energy you are putting into your sacred space. This energy is picked up—the one that is deep in your heart and soul.

Candles

Candles have been a part of humanity for thousands of years. They were (and still are!) used in almost every household. Most people have at least one candle at home in case of a power outage. Personally, I have many candles in my home. In my opinion, there is nothing better than lighting a candle at the end of the day for ambience, peace, and relaxation. Even if you have no intention of doing magic when lighting a candle, it will provide a sense of peace and tranquility, romance, and forgiveness.

When lit, candles are the embodiment of the fire element. Fire's energy is strong, with the courageous will to fight and make things right; these are the kinds of energies you are inviting in when you light a candle. Candle magic is honorable and straightforward, not to mention a much-needed component of most magical workings. I use candles in about 95 percent of my spells.

I have a drawer full of candles: all sizes, types, and, of course, colors. A candle's color is very important for any magical workings. Just as crystals, the planets, or the days of the week can influence your spellwork, the color of the candle you light signals your intent to the Universe, which is the essence of magic. When you purchase a candle, make sure that the inner color of the wax matches the outside color of the candle. You can verify this by flipping the candle over or asking the staff to help you find a candle that burns one color all the way through. If you choose a blue candle for a spell but, when you light it, it is white in the middle, it is not the right candle for any magical workings.

Another aspect of candle magic is the size and shape of the candle. There are votive candles, tealights, pillar candles, and more. Personally, I like to use tapered candles in my spells. These are long and thin, with a cylindrical base that narrows toward the top. When I light a candle for a spell, I prefer to let it burn until the flame consumes itself right at the end; if a candle is blown out, it loses its intent. Unfortunately, taper candles take hours and hours to burn down. The twelve-inch standard taper can burn for close to ten hours, but I don't expect you to wait that long for your tapered candles to consume. Try buying six-inch standard tapered candles (these burn for four hours), or the tiny four-and-a-half-inch tapers that burn for close to two hours. The sooner the candle consumes, the sooner you can get on with your day, and your home and mind will be safer for it.

Candles should never be left unattended at any time. Never leave candles lit when going to sleep; this is careless and a fire hazard to everyone around you. If you do not plan on being home all day but want to do some candle magic, it is best to use smaller candles. If you do have to leave a candle, it is always best to snuff the flame. A candle snuffer is a must! When doing candle magic, the flame cannot be blown out—it should always be snuffed, as you don't want your intention to blow away.

Another part of candle magic is dressing the candle. Don't worry, you are not going to "dress it" in a T-shirt and hat; this phrase means to rub the candle with the spell's designated oil. (If you don't have the designated oil, you can always use olive oil.) We will talk more about ways to dress a candle in later chapters, but for now, it is important to note that a candle is divided into two parts. From the middle up, toward the wick, is called the North Pole, and from the middle down is called the South Pole. When dressing a candle, rub a bit of the oil on both of your hands. The right hand dresses the North Pole, spreading oil from the middle to the top of the candle, while the left hand dresses the South Pole of the candle.

Resins, Herbs, and Essential Oils

Magic has a smell, and all who practice it know it's a blend of wax and essential oils, dry and fresh herbs, resins, and flowers. To me, that is the scent of magic. Soon your sacred space will smell similar, depending on the essential oils you like and the last spell you did, or the last herbs and flowers in your mortar and pestle.

Resins are simply the viscous substance of a plant. The most popular ones are frankincense, myrrh, and dragon's blood. These are always good to have in your sacred space.

Herbs are essential for any magical work. They're used in mojo drawstring bags and magical baths, and, most importantly, burned on your censer.

Essential oils are extremely important for all magical work. Their essence is strong enough to send your positive affirmations to the Universe. I recommend sticking to the purple essence for your sacred space, so make sure you have essential oils such as lavender, violet, or even lilac.

Essential oils are incredibly potent and should never be applied directly to the skin. All essential oils must first be diluted with a carrier oil such as coconut, almond, or jojoba oil. If you prefer, you can buy essential oils that are already diluted; make sure to read the label on your essential oil carefully. I recommend buying undiluted oils so you can modify the carrier oil and the strength of your blend.

Some people are very allergic to essential oils, so if you have not worked with an oil before, dilute it and then apply it to a small patch of skin. Keep an eye out for allergic reactions. If it is safe for you to use, then you can integrate it into your spellwork.

You should also be aware of any pets while using essential oils. Just because they are safe for us to use doesn't necessarily mean they are safe for our pets to be around. Some essential oils are more harmful than others.[1] If you think your pet has ingested any essential oil, contact your veterinarian immediately.

Resin Incense Burner

A resin incense burner is one of the most popular items in magical practice. They are used to burn resins such as myrrh and frankincense. Resin incense burners are usually fire- and heatproof. You can use a small metal, brass, stone, or terracotta bowl. I have a little cast-iron burner that I use all the time. Cast iron provides a fireproof container for anything you wish to burn or smolder, such as herbs and resins.

Censer and Charcoal Tablets

Charcoal tablets are round black discs about the size of a quarter. You may decide to use charcoal tablets in your practice. To light a charcoal tablet, place the tablet between your thumb and forefinger.

---

1. See https://www.aspca.org/news/essentials-essential-oils-around-pets for more information.

Using a lighter, light the end of the tablet that is furthest away from your fingers. Right away you will see sparks. Quickly place it inside your censer. Once lit, the charcoal tablet becomes red-hot and can cause burns if it's dropped. Trust me, I've had a few drops (and a few burned fingers) over the years.

Let the entire tablet ignite, but do not inhale the initial smoke. Once the tablet is lit, you can add herbs or resins on top. Always start with small amounts so as not to cause the charcoal to lose its heat.

A charcoal tablet has about thirty to forty minutes before it dies out. When it does, it turns into gray ash, at which point it is safe to dispose of. I like to dispose of my ashes on the ground outside of my house.

If I am using a small fireproof bowl to hold a charcoal tablet rather than a censer, I tend to add sand or soil at the bottom before I place the lit charcoal tablet inside. This is an additional safety measure.

Scissors and Knife

You should have a pair of scissors in your sacred space in case you need to cut herbs, paper, or cloth. You may also wish to cut your herbs using a plain knife.

Some people keep a double-edged knife in their sacred space to metaphorically cut through negative energies; this is common in banishing spells. Knives can be dangerous, but there are knives made specifically for magical work that are not sharp; for example, selenite knives are an option.

Mortar and Pestle

This is a crucial item for your sacred space. A mortar and pestle are used to mix dry herbs together, and you can even crush resins and blend them together. I like using a wooden mortar and pestle, as the wood keeps the scent of the resins and herbs. With that being said, there are solid granite, marble, and even porcelain options.

Crystals

These extraordinary, beautiful pieces of nature are a must for any sacred space. Crystals connect your needs to the Universe. Use purple crystals to decorate your sacred space, such as amethyst, purple fluorite, ametrine, or even sugilite.

If you are new to crystals, they can be an expensive hobby. Crystals come in all shapes, colors, and sizes. Tumbled crystals are round and smooth to the touch; these are the most popular. There are also unpolished, or rough, crystals, which come straight from the source,

Mother Nature. Then there are the ones that are cut especially for jewelry. These are just a few of the ways crystals can be purchased. Regardless of the shape or feel of a crystal, its magical properties are the same. Visit a crystal shop and wander around; you might be surprised what types of crystals you are drawn to.

To start with, I recommend buying a clear quartz crystal, one that you like and feel comfortable using in your sacred space.

Vase

Having a purple vase in your sacred space is a must. You may even decide to paint a ceramic vase your favorite shade of purple, or with a unique vision or pattern.

You could leave the vase empty, but keeping fresh flowers in your sacred space is always welcoming. Purple flowers would be ideal, but use what is available.

Empty Bottles, All Sizes

When you practice magic, you'll find a need for all sorts of bottles. Glass bottles are preferred, but recyclable plastic bottles are fine as well. Perhaps you need to store leftover herbs, flowers, or incense mixtures. If you complete a money spell, for example, the remaining herbs, resins, or even flowers can be reused.

Call this collection of empty bottles your stash. And let me tell you, you are going to have a lot to stash. In time, you will probably end up purchasing a shelf to put all your bottles on.

Cloth Color Patches
Cloth patches are good to have, preferably in a variety of colors. It is a good idea to start collecting small squares of different colors and fabrics in case a spell calls for something to be wrapped and buried.

Broom
As I said before, spiritual cleaning is very important. A broom clears spiritual dust and negative energies, and it also represents the feminine aspect of the home. You can still get straw brooms; do not use anything synthetic.

Magic Stationary
Magical stationary is used when things need to be written and later burned. This is common in spellwork. The word *stationary* may make this sound fancy, but it can just be colored pens and paper. For my magical stationary, I typically use

black and blue pens, colored pencils, and parchment paper. You may wish to use special paper or writing utensils, but it's not necessary.

Cushions or a Comfortable Chair

I like to have a sitting area in my sacred space; I often sit and reflect on what I am doing. And as I mentioned before, many people become so comfortable in their sacred space that they enjoy hanging out there even when they're not doing magic. I recommend adding a chair, cushions, or even pillows to your sacred space. Purple cushions would be great—the more you have, the cozier you will be.

Consecrating Your Sacred Space

Once you have everything you need for your sacred space, take some time to arrange it in a way that is pleasing to you. Then, before you can begin making magic, you will need to consecrate/bless the space where you will be doing your spells. It's always good to start by blessing your space to cleanse any energies left over from the last spell.

To bless your sacred space, light a charcoal tablet. Once it is ready, add one frankincense tear, then another. My mother, *la bruja* ("the witch"), as we fondly called her, told me that for magical workings, the more smoke there is, the better. She was right! My only piece of advice with that is to be aware of your smoke alarms.

Next, dress one white candle and three purple candles with olive oil. After you light them, watch them flicker while visualizing the strength needed for your magical journey.

Take your censor and its sacred smoke around the room in a clockwise motion, inviting the smoke to bless your new space, while saying:

Take this smoke to those that make dreams come true
My sacred space will be a place of positive
energy for the good of all, make it so

Let the candles burn out, and dispose of the charcoal ash in a safe manner.

Now that your sacred space has been blessed, you can start making magic! Return to this cleansing method in between spells.

Part I
Rainbow Spells

For most of us, it has been embedded since childhood that there is a pot of gold at the end of the rainbow. However, we know now that rainbows are only a refractive occurrence, reflecting light from the sun to manifest the arch of colors. But let's forget about all the scientific things behind such a phenomenon and concentrate on the magical influence the colors of the rainbow can bring to our daily existence, and how we can connect them to our magical workings.

Not only does the rainbow have seven colors with their own magical, spiritual, and physical meanings, but so does every color in the spectrum. Each color vibrates at a specific wavelength frequency. The color we see depends on the light's wavelength. There are even wavelengths of light that we cannot see!

By connecting a specific color to your magical workings, you are enhancing your needs and manifesting a positive outcome. Understanding and knowing the meanings of the colors will help you start to embrace color to cause an effect.

Our world is an actual rainbow of many colors, but without the arch. We identify essential services by the color of the uniforms: yellow and red for the fire department, blue for police, white for a doctor's coat, green for the army, blue for the air force, and the navy in white. In our daily lives, most of us have colors we prefer for our clothes, furnishings, and even vehicles. And almost everyone has a favorite color, which likely has changed over time.

We are also beings of light, radiating colors that not many people can see. These colors are known as the human aura—the human energy field. The human aura radiates colors around our etheric body. These colors can then be spiritually translated to give a sense of an individual's personality. Most people have various colors in their aura, or various shades of one color, that may change over time.

There are also the chakras, light centers that reside within our spiritual bodies. We have dozens of chakras, but there are seven main chakras. These start at the base of the spine and finish at the top of the head. Each chakra has a corresponding color and spiritual and emotional meanings we can connect to our magical workings. When you incorporate the chakras in your magical practice, you can improve your self-esteem, mood, and happiness just by using color.

The good thing about the color spectrum is that there is always a color that can enhance our energy field. Color can be broken down into three groups.

Primary Colors: The foundation of all the colors in the spectrum. The primary colors are red, yellow, and blue.

Secondary Colors: The primary colors blended 50/50. To create the color orange, blend yellow and red; to create the color green, blend yellow and blue; and to create the color violet, blend red and blue.

Tertiary Colors: Primary and secondary colors that have been blended to formulate the rest of the colors in the spectrum.

A rainbow is represented by primary and secondary colors.

While there are lots of colors out there we can all identify, there are decillions of blends and shades that would be hard to name. Think about paint companies that have dozens of shades of the same color, each with a unique name. Part of the reason there are so many shades of one color is because each color can be made warmer or cooler. The warmer the color, the more red it contains, and the more blue it has, the cooler it is.

Humans are magnets for color; we attract their wavelengths like a moth to a flame. Colorful wavelengths can penetrate us and change our auric field; they can even influence our chakras. Knowing your colors and their meanings will help you understand why a specific color is used in a magical working, and it can even explain why you feel drawn to certain colors. Don't be afraid to experiment with color! Start with your clothes. Let your body and your senses pick the color of your outfit. Let's say you're feeling angry; anger is represented by the color red. If you wear cool-colored clothing such as pink or blue, the redness your aura is portraying diminishes, almost as if the color blue is permeating your etheric field like an open freezer. Alternatively, if you're doing a spell for inner strength, you're not going to use any cool colors; warm colors would infuse your magical workings with encouragement.

Utilize color for everything you want to have or achieve in life. When you combine color with other magical tools—a planet, a day of the week, herbs, flowers, candles, and even crystals—you start to create magic by moving stagnant energy, helping it flow more smoothly around you and cause an effect.

Have faith in the things you do. Trust the process as you send your needs to the Universe and all its forces.

Days of the Week and Planet Connections

Before we dive into spellwork, I want to briefly explain how the planets and days of the week can be incorporated into your magical practice.

The more scientists discover about our solar system, the more we know about a planet, such as its size, surface, and distance from Earth. For magical purposes, we do not need to know the science of the solar system. Instead, we are going to focus on the mystical, spiritual connection humans have with the Universe, a connection that is still present today, just as it was in the past.

You may notice that in magical work, the sun and moon are both referred to as planets. Technically, the sun is a star, and the moon is classified as a satellite. And then there's Pluto, which used to be recognized as a planet in our solar system but has since been downgraded to a dwarf planet. With that being said, most magical practitioners think of the planets as celestial bodies.

Each of the planets in our solar system has its own attributes, according to planetary charts that are as old as time. These traits influence the days of the week they govern. Each planet is dedicated to specific tasks that we can tap into on a particular day of the week.

The days of the week work in conjunction with the planets:

Sunday: Day of the sun

Monday: Day of the moon

Tuesday: Day of Mars

Wednesday: Day of Mercury

Thursday: Day of Jupiter

Friday: Day of Venus

Saturday: Day of Saturn

There are three other major planets in our solar system that were discovered much later, so they do not have a corresponding day of the week; they are Pluto, Neptune, and Uranus. Just like the other celestial bodies, they have their own specific strengths. Each of these planets has a unique energy that you can tap into at any time.

Write which planet corresponds with the days of the week on your calendar until you know which day works with which planet. This information can—and should!—be applied to your magical practice. I love working with the days of the week and the planets; it gives my magic a little extra "get-up-and-go" energy, sending my spells into the cosmos with a boost.

2

Red

Red is the color of passion and lust. It ignites our urges and desires and enhances our sexuality. Red can be used in magic to give a spell strength. It also brings out the courageous spirit within all of us. Red amplifies the need to succeed. It empowers you to confront others if they have done you wrong, and it encourages you to stand up for yourself.

Everyday Uses of Red

Red enhances power and gives strength to your magical workings. Light a red candle when you need answers from others or the strength to face a difficult situation.

Wear red when you need energy to finish the day and to feel whole again. Too much red can cause anger and ignite resentful tendencies, but not enough red can make us manipulative, needy, and possessive.

RED COLOR MAGIC

This section shares some of my favorite simple spells, all powered by the magic of red.

A CRYSTAL FOR EVERLASTING LOVE

Set two red tiger's eye crystals on the grass under a full moon. Let them charge overnight. Give one to the person you love. Leave the other under your pillow. Forevermore, there will be love between the two of you.

A LOVE CHARM

If you want love to find you, keep the seeds of an apple you have eaten inside your shoes.

STRENGTH FOR A FRIEND

Hold the hand of a friend that needs your strength. With eyes closed, visualize a red flash of light penetrating your friend's heart. This will give them the strength they need to fight.

A HOMEMADE SECURITY SYSTEM

Using a red ribbon, hang a head of garlic behind the front door of your home.

Planet: Mars

Attributes: Courage, Leadership,
Passion for Life, Lust

This brave and competitive planet brings out an energy that lays dormant within each of us. We all want to possess Mars' spirit of courage and leadership. Mars incites. It inspires passion and the hunger to live life to the fullest. This planet is intelligent and competitive; it loves to use intellect as a biological weapon to win arguments.

Mars is a fighter. It fights for children and love; it fights against injustice. Mars is brutal and genuine. It helps you fight for your position in life. This planet doesn't understand people's reluctance not to go for the things they want, so it does everything in its power to make sure you shoot for the stars.

Mars is also about winning and persuasion. When you channel Mars' energy, you become a convincing speaker who makes sure people understand and agree with everything you are saying.

Day of the Week: Tuesday

Tuesday is the Mars day of the week. When you channel the energy of Mars on a Tuesday, you will feel as if you can conquer anything you set your mind to. Unlike the sun, who is gentle with its strength, Mars is a straightforward planet of leadership, strength, and courage, making Tuesday the perfect day to combat nasty, negative energies with force and conviction. Mars is on your side; this red planet makes us stronger and more capable so that we fight for what we believe in.

Don't be shy about harnessing this powerful energy. Together, Mars, Tuesday, and the color red are here to inspire you to become a more confident and poised individual. Having the strength to investigate life without fear is something we can all benefit from. Know that you have this color, planet, and day of the week supporting you and your wildest dreams.

Red Spells with Mars on Tuesdays

I like to use the energy of Mars to fight negative energies and complete tasks I've been procrastinating. Since Tuesday is the day of Mars, it is the perfect day of the week to get rid of the things or people in your life that no longer serve you. Tuesday, the planet Mars, and the color red help us handle even the most stressful situations. Incorporating red into your magic makes spells a lot stronger, as red enhances power. It also gives us strength to fight against the odds and the courage to pursue our dreams. The color red helps us endure physical pain, battles depression, and boosts emotional well-being and strength.

A Spell for Courage

Each of us has a courageous spirit, though we may prefer to be cautious. At one point or another, we will all face a situation where our courage leaps into action and sparkles. For me, it was the day I jumped in a car rolling down a hill because there were three children inside.

I had parked at a grocery store and was heading inside when I noticed a car parked illegally near the front door of the supermarket. There were three children inside, all under the age of five, if I had to guess. They were jumping on the car's seats. All of a sudden, I saw the car move. It was going backward, slowly at first, but then it began to pick up speed. I looked around the parking lot, but no one else seemed to notice, so I quickly approached the car. Thank goodness the driver's door was unlocked! I jumped in without a thought about the danger I could be placing myself in; my only concerns were for the children and the busy intersection at the bottom of the hill. I set the hand brake as the kids looked on; they had no clue why a stranger was in their car. Then I hurried inside the grocery store and spoke to the manager, and he took it from there.

This incident taught me that caution goes out the window when there is danger involved. In those moments, our courageous spirit surfaces and shines. The armed forces, police, and firefighters do similar heroic things every day. They find themselves in dangerous situations that give them little time to think—they must act. Instant courage is needed. But for most of us, courage is not about life or death. Everyday courage may be trying to find the harmony within, admitting something that is troubling you, or releasing something you've been holding on to.

When you need a little courage, perform this spell.

1. Set three red candles and one yellow candle in your sacred space. On all of the candles, use a pin to write a few words about the courage you need.

2. In a small bowl, add a teaspoon of olive oil and a table-spoon of poppy seeds. Mix well together, then dress your candles with this mixture while thinking of the courage you wish to have.

3. Once you have dressed all four candles, light them.

4. Take a garnet crystal. Use whatever dressing was left-over to anoint the garnet. Hold it in your hand and visualize the courage you need. Then place the garnet in front of the candles. With your hands, wave the candles' flames toward the crystal, visualizing that energy penetrating the crystal.

5. After all the candles have burned themselves out, hold the crystal in your hands for a moment, then place it in a red drawstring bag or piece of red material. Carry it with you all the time; the courage you seek will come to be.

The candle stubs can be tossed in the bin. Once you find your courage, empty the drawstring bag. Keep the garnet. Cleanse it, then reuse it in another spell, if needed.

A Spell for Leadership

A good leader is one who does not profit or manipulate others for their own personal gain. A good leader directs others unselfishly in all sorts of different settings, be it politics, religion, the workplace, or at home. If you are having difficulty communicating what is best for your family, your employees, or even yourself—or if you need help delegating in a leadership situation with integrity, empathy, and fairness—this spell can help.

1. On a Tuesday, dress a red and a blue candle using diluted rose geranium essential oil.

2. Light the candles with thoughts of leadership. Visualize yourself as a fair and just leader.

3. While the candles are burning, grab a piece of paper and a red pen. List the leadership qualities you want to have. Write down everything you wish to achieve as a leader; be as specific or as broad as you need. If you have a specific situation in mind, describe the ideal outcome.

4. Once you've finished writing, leave the piece of paper in front of the candles until they consume to the end.

5. Once the candles have burned out, take some red ribbon and the piece of paper to an oak tree. Holding the ribbon and paper in your hands, ask permission from the mighty oak. Say:

With your permission, I need your wisdom

6. Wait until you feel like you have been given permission; this could take a few minutes. The oak might grant permission via a sudden breeze or a falling leaf or acorn.

7. Once you have felt permission, wrap the piece of paper around a high branch, tying the red ribbon to keep it in place. Only take it down when you feel your leadership qualities are up to scratch.

This spell can be modified if you need courage or strength. Simply adjust steps two and three to reflect your needs.

A Spell for Passion

Occasionally, we fall back into mundane attitudes and lose the passion we had for life. This could be a passion for travel, seeing or doing new things, making new friends, or reviving something you once used to enjoy, like a musical instrument, sport, or craft.

To bring back the passion that once existed within you takes time. Most passions do not last forever; they are like a license you need to renew. It takes effort, but once your passion is reignited, you'll start to feel those tingly feelings again. If you miss feeling excited about an old passion of yours, try this spell.

1. Gather five hematite and five clear quartz crystals. Put them in a glass of water, then add a teaspoon of salt and a few drops of lavender essential oil. Leave them in the glass for about an hour.

2. After an hour has passed, tip the water out. Hold the crystals in your hands while visualizing the passion you want to reconnect to.

3. On a Tuesday, dress all in red and take the crystals out to your yard. This may be the same day you let the crystals soak, or it may be a few days later; try not to wait too long after soaking the crystals. (If you don't have a yard, you can finish the spell anywhere there is a lot of grass.)

4. If you are wearing shoes or socks, take them off so that your feet are bare. Then, walk around the grass, making a circle out of the crystals. Alternate placing hematite and clear quartz.

5. Stand in the center of the circle. Dig your feet and heels into the grass, grounding yourself with Mother Earth and connect-

ing to the energy of the crystals. Visualize yourself in a cone of energy; see the crystals' energies reaching into the sky above you.

6. Stand there with your feet firmly planted on the ground. Just enjoy the energy around you. After a few minutes, say:

Passion runs through me like the blood in my veins
I feel the strength of Mars deep within me
as I seek what once was
To resurface and stay forevermore

7. Pick up the crystals and rinse them in running water. Keep them on your altar and repeat this spell every Tuesday for three weeks in a row.

A Spell for Lust

Many of us have felt lust at some point. You may think back to the early days of a relationship that was once full of love and has now gone stale. Perhaps you remember sexual tension that was overwhelming until it was released.

As time passes, relationships stabilize, and we age, we tend to lose the intoxicating feeling of lust. Mars can help bring back that passion. Your feelings of passion may not be as strong as they once were, but they can still be potent enough to bring back the heat. To reignite feelings of lust, try this spell.

1. In your mortar and pestle, crush the following dry herbs: catnip, damiana, cloves, a pinch of cinnamon powder, and basil. Mix together.

2. Add a small piece of dragon's blood resin to the mix. Crush it together with the other herbs until you have a fine powder (or as close to powder as you can get).

3. Dress two red and two pink candles with diluted cinnamon essential oil. As you light them, wish for a lustful outcome. Visualize lust and feel it in your body. Welcome those sharp and familiar feelings once again. Think about a night of lustful passion, noticing the sparks in your body and senses.

4. Place the powder on top of a red cloth. Set it near the candles so that the powder can be charged by the flames. Leave the powder near the candles until they have burned out.

5. Sprinkle the powder on fresh sheets and pillowcases. Make sure you dust it away before going to bed. Enjoy a night of passion!

6. Keep the rest of the powder in the red cloth. Store under your pillow, by your bedside, or under the bed. Use again when needed.

A SPELL TO BANISH NEGATIVE ENERGY

Tuesdays are good days to rid of negative energy and workings, whether intentional or unintentional. Sometimes we walk into a place and immediately know there has just been an argument or someone has been badmouthing someone else—it may have been you. Or perhaps you enter a space and can just feel the stagnate energy in the room. Here is a spell to repel negative energy.

1. In a red drawstring bag, place basil, crushed bay leaves, a clear quartz crystal, and three rusty, small nails. Cinch the bag shut.

2. Hold the bag in your hands and visualize it repelling any and all negative energy around you.

3. Whenever you carry the drawstring bag with you, you'll be protected from negative energies.

Planet: Pluto

Attributes: Surrender, Transformation, Revelation

The color red works well with Mars *and* Pluto. Pluto utilizes a darker shade of red: I like to call it *volcanic red*. Pluto can bring out the worst or the best in people, but we are going to acknowledge Pluto's good traits.

Pluto helps us release our ego-driven nature and surrender our unattractive character traits to become more grounded with those around us. Pluto fights in the name of love and eliminates the swamp of unwanted emotions from our systems for good. If you truly want to change, Pluto will help you achieve the transformation you desire.

Pluto creates, but it can also destroy. Therefore, work with this planet to get rid of any negative energy sent your way, such as jealousy, spite, or greed.

Day of the Week: Tuesday/Saturday

As an outer planet, Pluto is not associated with any day of the week; it was discovered after the days of the week were assigned to particular planets. I like to assign Pluto to Tuesdays for its courage and fairness, but I also work with Pluto on Saturdays when getting rid of negative energy.

RED SPELLS WITH PLUTO ON TUESDAY OR SATURDAY

The hidden always comes out when Pluto is around. If you want the truth, Pluto will bring it to the surface. With Pluto's help, you may find the end to a problem or a lovely new beginning. This planet will explore your situation and find ways to accommodate your needs. Pluto sheds light on confusing situations, whether they have to do with relationships, work, or family members.

A SPELL FOR HONESTY

White lies are often told in an attempt not to hurt someone's feelings, whereas serious lies are told to inflict pain, sorrow, and emotional upset. A lot of the time, liars appear credible, but you may know in your heart that someone is being dishonest.

The first thing you need to do is take a deep breath and release your frustration. Then ask yourself if it's worth confronting this person. Do you have the emotional stillness it will take to do so? If you don't, a confrontation may turn into an altercation that cannot be resolved. Instead, try this spell.

1. Get a white candle. With a pin, carve the name of the person you believe to be spreading lies into the wax.

2. Take two red candles. Using a pin, write "the truth shall be known" on one candle. On the other candle, write the same name you carved on your white candle.

3. In a small bowl, mix half a teaspoon of black crushed peppercorns and a full teaspoon of olive oil. Mix well.

4. Dress the red candles with this mixture while saying:

No harm shall fall upon the liar
But the truth must be heard

5. Dress the white candle with plain olive oil while saying:

Surrender to the truth and admit to the lies
Make people see who you really are

6. Sprinkle black pepper around the candles and let them consume. Once they have finished burning, lies will be refuted and the truth will be known.

A Spell for a Personality Adjustment

There is no denying we all have sides of our personality we don't particularly like. Perhaps you think you talk too much, are too judgmental, are overly critical of others, or do not have the patience to handle everyday stressors. If you have an aspect of your personality that you would like to improve, try this spell.

1. Print out a picture of yourself. Place it on a dark red cloth in your sacred space. On the back of the picture, write down what you wish to adjust.

2. Flip the picture over so that it is faceup. Place a handful of pine nuts and lavender buds on top.

3. Dress a red candle with olive oil. As you do so, visualize what is needed (or what you would like less of).

4. Let the candle consume to the end. Once it has burned out and cooled, roll up the red cloth and all its contents. Keep it under your pillow, on your bedside table, or under the bed. Soon you will notice your personality shifting; you will exhibit more of what you like and less of what you don't.

A Spell for Protection

Believe it or not, it is very easy to absorb negative energy. Absorbing negativity is even easier when it is directed to an individual, and negative energy is at its strongest when someone is trying to manipulate your essence with a part of you, like a strand of your hair or anything else they can get their hands on. This is negative magic, and it is meant to inflict pain or sorrow.

The more we think about someone practicing negative magic and directing it at us, the more we open ourselves to those thoughts, and—unfortunately—the more negative energy penetrates us. But we can break this toxic cycle and protect ourselves from negativity with a simple spell.

1. Set three red candles in your sacred space. Squeeze a fresh lime. Place the juice in your hands and dress the candles while visualizing the protection you are seeking.

2. Once all three candles have been dressed, light them.

3. Light a charcoal tablet on your censer. Add a few flakes of dragon's blood.

4. Run a tiger's eye crystal and an obsidian crystal over this sacred smoke. (If you are doing this spell for more than one person, you will need both crystals for each person you are

protecting.) As you run the crystals over the smoke, say the name of the person that the crystals are for.

5. Carefully take your censer around your home, letting the smoke engulf each room. When I say each room, I mean it—don't forget to take it into the bathroom too. Lastly, open the front door while holding the censer. Say:

Protected my home is

6. Take the censer to the back door. Open it and say:

And straight out the back door you will leave
Causing no harm to those I love the most

If you do not have a back door, use a back window. If there is no other option, you can stay at the front door.

7. Once you've finished walking the smoke through your home, snuff the candles. Relight them every day for seven days or until they are consumed right to the end.

8. Give everyone you protected with this spell their tiger's eye and obsidian crystals. Ask them to keep them nearby until the candles have burned themselves out.

A Spell to Break a Hex

It is inevitable that we will experience periods of life where things are not going well for us. When you feel your emotional life force diminishing, when it feels like everything around you is collapsing, when things break for no reason, when relationships are tested, when finances are dwindling faster than you can replenish them—you are being targeted by a negative energy force that needs to be stopped.

If you know who is responsible for the negative energy in your life, you can address it in this hex-breaking spell. Even if you don't know who is responsible, you can still address the source of the negative energy in this spell. This is one of the easiest ways to break a hex.

1. In a bowl, place a cup of salt. Add red food coloring and mix it together until you have dark red salt. Let it dry out in the sun. Only when the red salt is dry can you move on to the next step of the spell.

2. Find a handheld mirror. Ideally, it should be the size of an iPad. Keep in mind that you must be able to smash the mirror at the end of this spell.

3. When you are home alone, move around the house with this mirror. Holding the glass facing

away from you, capture every wall, every nook and cranny. Make sure the mirror does not capture any bit of you, not even your toes. While you walk, chant out loud. Say:

Mirror in my hands, capture all evil from my home

4. Once you have captured the whole house in the mirror, go to your front door. Place a red cloth on the ground. Place the mirror faceup on the cloth, making sure you are not seen in the mirror. Get a heavy object, like a rock or a brick, and throw it at the glass until it smashes into tiny little pieces. Be very careful as you do this so that you do not hurt yourself.

5. Take your bowl of red salt and sprinkle the salt on the smashed mirror while saying:

Evil shall no longer lurk in my home
It is now shattered, never to return

6. Wrap everything up in the red cloth, including every piece of glass and whatever is left of the mirror. Toss the bundle into the bin, never to be seen again.

7. Vacuum the space where the mirror was to get every last shard of glass.

3

Orange

Orange is a secondary color, a blend of yellow and red. Yellow and red have their own powerful meanings, and when blended, they create a cheerful, gracious color that attracts warmth and love for all who harvest its energy.

I like to think orange is a clever color. It challenges the mind and boosts concentration. Orange also invites in the freedom you have always sought and helps apply it to your daily life. The color orange can help you express your deepest thoughts; it opens lines of communication, especially with the spirit world. Ultimately, orange brings happiness—unexpected gifts and things you never thought possible arrive in your life when you invite in orange's energy and glow.

Everyday Uses of Orange

Orange is the color that honors words spoken, so it is great to wear in your place of employment. You can light an orange candle to improve communication or to meet new friends. Wearing orange can also help you remember things you seem to forget. It is a very positive color and provides encouragement when needed.

ORANGE COLOR MAGIC

In magic, orange is the color of growth, warmth, wisdom, learning, and happiness.

TO ATTRACT MONEY

Simple but effective: carry orange honeysuckle in your purse or wallet. Replace once a month, ideally on a Sunday.

FOR A FRESH START

On a piece of orange paper, write about the fresh start you are wishing for—the more detail, the better. Once you're done, burn the letter. Then collect the ashes and blow them toward the sea. If you don't live by the seaside, a river or another large body of water is fine.

Make sure to do this on a windy day so the ashes can reach the forces where fresh starts are born.

To Help with Decision Making

Light an orange candle. While it is burning, meditate about the situation to find the decision that is in your best interest. You'll decide before midnight.

For Bravery

When you need a little extra strength to face a challenge, make a hole in an orange and place an aquamarine crystal deep inside. Keep this orange in your room for two weeks. Every day before you leave your house, hold the orange in your hands and wish for the bravery you need, and you shall find it. After the two weeks are up, dispose of the orange, but keep the aquamarine so it can be used in another spell.

A Spell for an Overloaded Mind

1. Place two orange tapered candles in your sacred space.
2. Pour half a teaspoon of olive oil into one hand, then gently spread the oil on your palms. Pick up one candle at a time

and dress them with the oil. As you do this, visualize your mind becoming as clear as water.

3. After you've finished dressing the candles, place them in candleholders and light them. As you do, visualize everything that is on your mind melting away just like the flames melt the wax.

4. Stand in front of the candles for a few moments. Breathe in the color orange from your candles' flames. Say:

> **Clear as water my mind will be**
> **Today, tomorrow, and until I need it to be**

5. Let the candles burn themselves out.

A SPELL FOR WISDOM

1. Go to your altar/sacred space and light an orange candle.

2. Light a charcoal tablet. Place a few dry rosemary leaves on top. Keep adding leaves to the tablet as it burns so that there are always fresh rosemary leaves on top. Let the smoke be present all around you. Visualize the wisdom needed to make the right decision.

3. Stay in your sacred space for a while. Lounge around on a cushion or sink into a comfortable chair. Close your eyes and visualize yourself where you want to be. See yourself having the wisdom to get there.

4. Let the candle and tablet burn themselves out.

A SPELL TO LEARN NEW SKILLS

1. Cut a piece of orange material to be three inches by three inches. Lay it flat.

2. On top of the material, place a walnut, a yellow calcite crystal, and a copper coin—a penny will do. Make a little bundle out of this. Use a piece of leather or ribbon to tie the bundle closed.

3. Prepare a charcoal tablet in your sacred space. Once it's lit, place two frankincense resin drops on top.

4. Wave your bundle over this cleansing smoke. As you do, visualize the skills you need or want to learn.

5. Keep this bundle on your person until you feel you are easily learning new skills. Then empty the bundle and dispose of its contents, but keep the crystal and the coin. Redo the spell as needed.

Uranus

Attributes: Future, Rebellion, Change, Breakthroughs

Uranus is a risk-taking planet; radical changes are this planet's forte. You can use this planet's energy to cause an effect, to change your life, and to shake up the way you do things.

Uranus rules both the very ancient and the very modern. It also rules the future, so it can help you see beyond the ordinary. This planet stimulates ideas and is the mastermind of invention. Its motto is "Nothing is fixed that is changeable." It likes helping humanity grow through innovation, especially technology. Because Uranus is all about sparking invention and investigation, we can use this planet's energy when we want to change our place of employment or find a new position within a company or firm.

Uranus, like the other outer planets, was never assigned a day of the week, so you can do these spells anytime.

ORANGE SPELLS WITH URANUS

Uranus is included in the orange chapter, although it is often associated with the color teal, which is a combination of green and blue that expresses growth and encourages us to speak up when needed. Teal also enhances spiritual balance when it comes to growth and development. However, Uranus's other main color is rust orange, and most of the Uranus spells in the following section use this color. Now, rust orange is a very evocative color; it is the color of autumn and the color of rusty nails, which are used for protection in magic. Together, rust orange and teal pacify Uranus's intensity and can reveal what the future has in store for us.

A SPELL FOR ENCOURAGEMENT

When we lack the courage to pursue our goals, it could be because we are frightened of the outcome. Try this spell when you need to be encouraged to make some changes in life.

1. Set a citrine crystal outside, preferably in your yard. If you don't have a yard, place the crystal inside a potted plant, on top of the soil, on your balcony or porch. The energies of the elements should cleanse the crystal for three days.

2. On the third day, prepare a little orange pouch using a drawstring bag. (You could also make your own from orange material.) Inside the pouch add a teaspoon of shell-less sunflower seeds, one peppercorn, and a teaspoon of orange zest.

3. Recover your citrine and hold it in your hands. Visualize the encouragement needed. Then place it inside your orange pouch.

4. Take your orange encouragement pouch to your sacred space. Light a white tealight candle and leave your pouch in front of it until the candle expires on its own.

5. Carry this little pouch with you during the day. At night, you can place it under your pillow, by your bedside, or under the bed.

6. After seven days, empty the contents of the pouch in the bin. Keep the crystal for another spell or reuse it if you decide to do the spell again.

A SPELL TO DISPEL UNWANTED SPIRITS FROM YOUR HOME

Spirits come and go from our homes more often than you'd think. They typically enter a home out of curiosity, but they eventually move on. Unfortunately, there are some spirits that do not want to leave, for whatever reason, and end up sticking around. If they have nothing to offer but negativity, that is something your home doesn't want or need. This spell can send spirits away.

1. Go to a hardware store and pick up twenty of the largest nails you can get your hands on. Preferably, they should have a head and a pointed end.

2. When you get them home, place the nails in a bowl. Add a cup of vinegar, a generous splash of hydrogen peroxide, and a tablespoon of salt. Stir the mixture and let the nails sit in it until they oxidize and the liquid becomes an off color. When this happens, your nails are ready to use.

3. Cut four five-by-five inch squares of red material. Cut one five-by-five inch square of orange material.

4. In each red square, place five nails facing the same direction. Wrap them up tightly. To keep them in place, wrap black ribbon around the bundle. As you tie each bundle closed, say:

My home is protected, and no entity will penetrate it

5. Once you have finished making your red bundles, put one bundle inside the four corners of your home, with the points of the nails facing the outside of the home. (If your house is

square, finding the home's four corners will be easy. Otherwise, sketch a diagram of your floorplan to determine the four corners of your home.)

6. When finished, grab the square of orange cloth and dip it in the nail's water solution. There's no need for it to be soaked, but make sure the cloth is damp. Take this cloth to your front door and wipe it down, saying:

> **Rust protects those I love and my**
> **home from unwanted entities**
> **That are trying to come in the front door**

7. If you have a back door or side doors, repeat step six with each door.

8. Bottle whatever water solution is left over. Use it one more time, exactly seven days later, on your front door. Keep the leftover water solution for as long as needed. After three months, redo this spell again and start the solution from scratch.

A SPELL FOR A NEW JOB

Having complete faith in yourself allows you to tackle anything you set your mind to. There is nothing that can stop you from starting an exciting new chapter of your life. When you're ready for a new role, or even an entirely different career, try this spell.

1. You will need two orange and two teal candles. Dress the candles with diluted orange essential oil. As you do, visualize the job you want to have. Think about the kinds of tasks you would do day to day. Don't discount your present employment, as there might be possibilities you haven't thought about before.

2. When you finish dressing the candles, spread out baking paper. Sprinkle the paper with poppy seeds and gently roll the candles in them. Some may stick, some may not, but the poppy seed essence will roll on.

3. Get a red jasper crystal and a clear quartz crystal. Rub them with diluted orange essential oil, then hold them in your hands and spend more time thinking about your dream job. Where is it? Do you have an office space? What is the atmosphere like?

4. Place the candles in a circle, then light each candle. As you do, visualize a new work environment, one where you feel comfortable and where you will excel.

5. Place the crystals in the middle of the candles and say:

> **There is a company out there looking for someone like me**
> **Guide them to me**

6. Let the candles consume.

7. Going forward, keep the two crystals with you at all times. Be open-minded about opportunities. Soon, you will come across the perfect job, and it will bring you a new start.

8. Once you find that new job, take the crystals and rinse them under water to cleanse them. Use them again if you ever need to redo this spell, or feel free to use them in another spell.

A SPELL TO CALM TURMOIL

Experiencing turmoil is like cooking a pot of soup—and you are the pot. You hold everything the cook throws inside you: different spices, vegetables, and stock until you are full to the brim. You are caught in the soup of life. But you need to be more like the ladle.

The ladle goes in the soup, but it comes back out! And it doesn't stay in the pot while the soup is cooking. So, let's embody the ladle and remove ourselves from life's turmoil. To do that, we are making make-believe soup.

1. Go to a toy store and purchase a pot and a ladle. Make sure to get the metal ones, those that look like the real thing.

2. Set these cooking props in your sacred space. Tie an orange bow around the ladle.

3. Add as much water to the little pot as it will hold.

4. Balance the ladle on top of the pot, but don't let it fall into the water. If you must use glue to keep it in place, do so. Once the ladle is balanced, say:

There will be no more turmoil in my home
As clear as this water is, my daily stressors disappear
Without reaching a boiling point

5. Place the pot and ladle in the kitchen. Set them somewhere high up so they will not be disturbed. Change the water every week. This will ensure you keep the peace and avoid slipping back into turmoil.

4
Yellow

Yellow is a very psychic color. It's the color of the intuitive chakra, the solar plexus. The color yellow inspires us to listen to our gut feelings, makes us more sensitive to others' feelings and emotions, and opens our minds to new possibilities, often via our dreams.

Yellow brings happiness to the home. It's also a color of intelligence. This makes it an excellent color to decorate with if you frequently study at home, as it helps you absorb knowledge like a plant needing water. If you live with children, make sure to have yellow objects around, as they have ever-growing minds.

Everyday Uses of Yellow

Use yellow to boost your mood and the mood of everyone around you. If you are having trouble accessing your gut feelings, wear yellow to tap into your intuition. Next time you buy a piece of clothing for children, choose something yellow. Wearing yellow will help them grasp as much as they can in their early learning years.

Too much yellow can make us overly critical and unwilling to listen to anyone else, but not enough yellow can make us timid, afraid to learn, and unmotivated.

YELLOW COLOR MAGIC

When you use the color yellow in your spells, it will help you manifest anything you desire. Yellow carries our messages of hope to the Universe with the help of the air element.

TO REDUCE STRESS

Have a cup of chamomile tea if you need to de-stress before a big event.

To Invite in Money

If you need money, sprinkle chamomile flowers inside your wallet or handbag.

To Ensure a Fun Gathering

If you're throwing a party and want to make sure everyone has a good time, add two drops of lime essential oil and three drops of sweet orange essential oil to a diffuser to make a citrus punch. By the end of the night, people will be asking when you are going to have another get together.

To Encourage Learning

Light yellow candles when children are doing homework or when you are studying for something.

For Luck at Every Turn

Always have yellow candles at home. Light them before trying your luck or whenever you want to invite in lucky energy.

To Be Understood

Light an orange and yellow candle when you feel like others are not understanding you. This will invite in clear communication.

When You Need to Apologize

If you need to apologize to someone you've hurt, make sure to bring a bouquet of white and yellow flowers with you. The apology you are offering will be accepted.

Planet: Sun

Attributes: Learning, Happiness, Healing, Strength, Financial Stability

When we go to bed at night, we trust that the sun will be there in the morning, shining down on our homes as it has done for eternity. Even if it's cloudy or stormy and we cannot see the sun, it is still there, watching over us from behind the clouds. It's easy to forget how important the sun is in our day-to-day lives; we could not live without it. I suppose you could say the sun and the moon are the only things we can truly depend on during our time on this plane of existence.

The sun is the warrior, the hunter, the protector. It represents the masculine energy within all of us. People often speak of getting in touch with their feminine side, but we mustn't forget to tune in to our masculine side as well.

The sun is always in constant motion, albeit slowly. It leads us through the seasons, reminding us that no matter how many times we need to start fresh in life, we will move on eventually—some of us faster than others. The sun teaches us resiliency so that we can spring back to life when the time is right.

The warmth that shines in each of us is powered by the sun. The sun brings heat, but it also brings us to our boiling point at times. If you find ways to positively harness the sun's energy, you'll have a new lease on life. The sun is the courageous spirit within that inspires us to do the things we are scared of. Perhaps this is something mundane, like changing our career or studying extra hard to attain something we want, or perhaps it is something more extreme, like bungee jumping or getting on a roller coaster even though it scares the hell out of us.

Day of the Week: Sunday

The sun brings people together by exploring the family nucleus for a better understanding of each other's needs. Sunday, the day of the sun, is the perfect day to perform magic that has to do with growth and financial stability. Carry out money and healing spells—not only for physical ailments, but spiritual ones too.

Utilize Sundays to find the strength within. Don't be afraid to believe in yourself. Even if something you want to achieve feels out of reach at the time, it won't be forever. When you embody the sun, shyness and fear cannot get in your way. Talk to someone you trust about everything you want to accomplish in life. Speak it into existence!

YELLOW SPELLS WITH THE SUN ON SUNDAYS

We associate the sun with the color yellow. Not only does the sun provide courage and strength, it also promotes learning at every age, just like yellow does. When we combine yellow, Sundays, and the sun, something sparks deep within us and connects us to our intuition, which we tend to brush off most of the time.

A SPELL FOR KNOWLEDGE

Knowledge comes from applying yourself to learn, and learn you will. Try this spell.

1. On a Sunday morning, dress two yellow candles with oil. As you do, think of the wisdom you or someone you love needs at this moment.

2. Once you've finished dressing the candles, place them in your sacred space. Light the candles, then ignite a charcoal tablet. Place a few dry leaves of rosemary and spearmint on the tablet.

3. Let this smoke fill you with a sense of knowledge, activating brain waves in you or the person who needs it. Think of this activated part of the brain as an area that was dormant and needs to come to life.

4. On a piece of yellow paper, draw this activated part of the brain that is open to assimilating knowledge. This does not have to look like an actual brain—just have fun! Perhaps it is just a drawing of a circle. Within the brain you have drawn, write all the letters of the alphabet and the numbers one to ten.

5. Set your pen down. On top of the yellow paper, place a citrine crystal, a few drops of rosemary essential oil, a few corn kernels, and a single walnut. Fold the yellow piece of paper around these items, wrapping it up as small as you can.

6. Place your folded paper in a yellow drawstring bag and cinch it closed. Wave the bundle over the smoke a few times, still visualizing the knowledge you wish to acquire or the knowledge your loved one needs. If the smoke has started to dissipate, add more rosemary leaves to the charcoal tablet.

7. Keep this knowledge bundle close to you, or place it wherever you study. If you made the bundle for someone else but don't want them to know, hide it somewhere in the vicinity of where they study. Make sure to dedicate it to them saying their name out loud.

8. After a month has passed, dispose of the contents inside the drawstring bag. Repeat the spell as needed.

A SPELL FOR FINANCIAL STABILITY

One good thing about the sun is it knows and understands today's financial needs, but keep in mind that the sun never rewards us when we are being greedy. Oftentimes when doing money magic, the more you ask for, the less you end up getting. This might be because you were concentrating on your financial stability instead of the endless possibilities around you. This spell is all about enhancing your financial stability through new avenues.

1. Dress two green candles, one yellow candle, and one orange candle with diluted lavender essential oil. While you do so, think of financial stability and visualize what it means to you. Some may visualize a house, a wallet full of money, or spending money, but don't limit yourself to only that. You could visualize a car, a new wardrobe, or whatever financial stability means to you.

2. Once you've finished dressing your candles, place a yellow cloth in your sacred space. In a small bowl, add a teaspoon of uncooked rice, a teaspoon of dry basil, and a teaspoon of oats. Mix them together, then sprinkle the mixture over the yellow cloth, keeping your financial stability in mind the entire time.

3. Place the four candles on the cloth in the shape of a circle. The two green candles should be facing each other. Light the candles. Visualize the candles' flames fusing with the yellow cloth. Say:

> **My financial needs are simple**
> **Let this rice grow with my needs**
> **Let the basil bring me luck**
> **And let the oats find magical ways for**
> **me to enhance and develop**
> **Show me a way I have not considered before**

4. Let the candles burn themselves out.

5. Once the candles have consumed, wrap up the yellow cloth so that the rice, basil, and oats are inside. Take the bundle to a prominent financial institution (perhaps the bank you use) late at night. Open the bundle and sprinkle the mixture on the front door when no one is watching. In a few days, your finances will begin to grow!

A Spell for Happiness

If you asked someone what they want most in life, they would probably say health and happiness. Many of us think everything has to be going well in our lives before we can say we are truly happy. But maintaining happiness is not as difficult as we make it.

1. Think of something that has brought happiness into your life. How did it make you feel at that time? Hold on to that feeling.

2. Go outside and look up at the sun. Ask the sun if your emotional well-being can shine just as brightly as the sun shines on you.

3. For the next week, every time you walk out of the house, smile. The sun is always shining, even if we can't see it behind the clouds, so smile even if you don't feel like it. Smile at the sun

so it knows you are trying, and in turn, it will shine down on you. Soon, you will start to feel happy again.

A Spell to Strengthen and Heal the Physical Body

It's no fun to be sick. The word *sick* means different things to different people. For some of us, *sick* means getting a cold or the flu. Others struggle with chronic health conditions, which can be debilitating. And there are the hard, life-threatening diagnoses we have to come to terms with.

In addition to conventional medicine, working magic or performing healing rituals can only benefit us. Magic can make us feel physically and emotionally stronger. But in order to move forward, we need to accept our illnesses. Then the healing process can begin. With the strength of the sun, anything is possible.

1. Dress four yellow candles with walnut oil. As you do so, think of the healing needed or accept the journey ahead.

2. In a brown paper bag, place the following fresh herbs: thyme, rosemary, angelica, and fennel. Add a small piece of a cinnamon stick, an amethyst crystal (preferably in a jewelry setting, such as a necklace or a ring), and a sprinkle

of nutmeg powder. As you add the items to the bag, continue thinking about the healing you need.

3. Gently shake the bag so that the items and herbs mix together, then set it down in your sacred space.

4. Place the candles around the paper bag, but don't place them too close, as this could be a fire hazard. Light the candles.

5. In a meditative state, visualize the candle flames penetrating the brown bag with the strength and courageous spirit of the fire element.

6. Reflect on how you arrived at this very moment. Take as long as you need. Feel yourself relax as you seek the sun's healing energies and its strength.

7. Let the candles burn right to the end. Once they have consumed, remove the amethyst crystal from the bag. Hold it in your hand and activate it. In other words, ask the crystal to help you with whatever is ailing you. Ask it to calm you, and to calm your illness. Once this is accomplished, if you used amethyst jewelry, put it on and wear it every day of your healing journey.

8. Place the paper bag's remaining items in a yellow drawstring bag. Carry the drawstring bag with you. Touch it or hold it

during trying times, thinking of the sun's energy giving you strength every step of the way.

9. You can do this healing spell as many times as needed—just replace the herbs you used with new ones.

A SPELL FOR STRENGTH

More often than not, when faced with a challenging situation, we are seeking emotional strength rather than physical strength. The sun's energy can help with that.

1. Get a clear quartz crystal, preferably in a jewelry setting, like a ring or a necklace. Take it outside and place it on the ground, making sure to set it somewhere it will get a lot of direct sunlight. Leave it outside until the sun sets.

2. Before you bring the crystal in, make a hot cup of black tea. Let the tea steep for a few minutes while you get the crystal.

3. Once the tea has cooled a bit, dunk the clear quartz crystal in the tea for a few seconds. Then hold the crystal in your hands and visualize the strength you need at this point in your life.

4. Pour the tea down the drain. Keep the crystal on you for as long as you need emotional strength and balance. When you start to feel your strength dwindling, do this spell again.

GOLD COLOR MAGIC

Unlike yellow, gold has a metallic luster to it. This color works with karma and your spiritual guides. It is perceptive, intuitive, creative, and peaceful.

Gold has more of a spiritual connotation than yellow. This color will never let you down, as it works with spirit. And because the color gold can calm the mind, it may even enable you to contact the spirit world.

Gold powers imagination and aids dream visualization. It can bring mental stability to the unfocused brain, making it an excellent color to use in meditation, groupwork, and spiritual self-development. It relieves stress in the home and works amazingly well as a sleep aid for young children.

Here are other ways to invite gold's gifts into your life.

To Send a Love Heart

Dip your index finger into honey and draw the shape of a heart on your chest. This will send a loving message to the object of your affection.

To Feel Beautiful

Take a few short pieces of straw, enough so that you have a small bundle, and tie pink and red ribbon around them. Keep the bundle with you to feel all the beauty you hold within and more.

When You Need Money

Place a few copper coins (pennies will do) in a small, clear bowl. Cover the coins with honey and sesame seeds. This will bring money to you.

Here's another easy way to attract riches: find some fake gold dust and sprinkle it in your front yard.

5
Green

Green is connected to nature and endless growth. Enjoy the colors of nature outside. Breathe in the greenery around you and let it feed your emotions so you can grow mentally, spiritually, and physically. There is nothing more rewarding than hugging a tree full of green, healthy branches; do it unashamedly. Seek nature's energy for whatever is troubling you.

The color green is also associated with money. It invites in luck and soothes difficult emotions. Light a green candle to call in money or to heal emotional pain.

Everyday Uses of Green

Green is a color of hope and understanding. It heals the heart from past emotional upsets and settles down emotional stress and grief. Work with the color green to manifest acceptance and peace. Blue and green are the main colors of our own habitat, which is always growing and changing. The color green reminds us that nothing in life is permanent—even nature changes with the seasons.

Green can bring peace, love, acceptance, and spiritual and financial growth. Too much green can lead to selfishness. If you feel surrounded by fear or lack self-love, add more green into your life to help with your emotional well-being.

GREEN COLOR MAGIC

Green is one of the best colors to work with because it has so many uses. It helps strengthen relationships, promotes growth, and ensures success. It's a very lucky color.

TO FIND AND KEEP FRIENDSHIPS

Keep a bloodstone in your handbag or wallet to make new friends that will last a lifetime.

To Have Two Hearts Beat as One

Crush a few fresh basil leaves with your hands. Use the oily substance to anoint the erogenous zones, such as your inner wrists, earlobes, the nape of the neck, or behind the knees. As your heart beats, it will send signals to the one you are in love with.

To Find a Job

Chop a bunch of parsley and add it to your bath. Visualize this herb guiding you toward the job you need. Once finished, throw the parsley in the bin and drain the bath. The job you seek will come your way.

To Spark Someone's Interest

To grab the attention of someone you like, carry the leaves of a willow tree in a small, green drawstring bag.

For Legal Proceedings

It's no fun going to court. Light a purple and green candle on a Thursday for good results.

For an Ego Adjustment

If someone has an ego problem, dress a green candle with olive oil. Write the name of the person on the candle using a pin. Then light the green candle in that person's name, and an ego adjustment will come their way.

To Attract Money
Light a green candle whenever possible. Send your money needs to the Universe as many times as you want!

To Sell Your Home
Light a green and yellow candle every Sunday until your house is sold.

For a Successful Business
Always have a green and orange candle burning in your place of business.

For Eternal Love
Place a few pink rose petals and fresh rosemary leaves in your shoes on a Friday, and you will be loved forever more.

Planet: Neptune

Attributes: Creativity, Music, Romance,
Psychic Gifts, Spirituality

The planet Neptune is all about inspiration. Neptune can inspire your deepest desires to come to fruition. As the great musician and composer of life, Neptune's creative expression often comes through writing, painting, sculpting, architecture, and music. Unsurprisingly, this planet is a bit of a romantic.

Neptune is sensitive to others' emotional well-being and facilitates connection to other realms of consciousness and higher energies. Receiving messages via dreams and enhancing psychic abilities are two of Neptune's gifts. Neptune is a very observant planet; it watches the world go by with patience and curiosity.

As an outer planet, Neptune does not have a day of the week assigned to it. You can work with Neptune's energies any time.

GREEN SPELLS WITH NEPTUNE

Interpreting dreams and enhancing psychic abilities can be aided by Neptune, as well as anything to do with romance.

WHEN YOU NEED TO CREATE, COMPOSE, OR WRITE

Sometimes, when we need to put words on paper, notes to music, or paint onto a canvas, we could sit in front of the computer, a musical instrument, or a blank canvas for hours and have nothing happen. In those moments, it feels like our imagination has abandoned us.

Over the years, I've found a few things that help with creativity, concentration, and artistic expression. Try any of these simple spells next time you're looking for inspiration.

- If you evoke Neptune before beginning a creative endeavor, you can't go wrong.

- Always have green or yellow candles burning while you are creating.

- Have a glass of water on your creative workstation. Visualize the water as an open canvas ready to be filled.

- I like to wear a feather on my head to let my thoughts fly to a place where creation exists. Sometimes I wear a blue or green bandana on my head to keep my creative side emotionally balanced.

- Music is the soul of any artist, so play music you love as often as possible. Music can balance your chakras, freeing up creative energy.
- Wear green clothing for inspiration.
- Burn leaves like rosemary or spearmint on your censer. It's also a good idea to have a few walnuts around your creative space.
- Crystals are great for any type of creative inspiration. Green or yellow crystals should always be around your working space.

A Spell to Romanticize a Dream

When we hear the word *romanticizing*, we often think of romance or physical pleasure. But romanticizing doesn't have to be about relationships. We can also romanticize our dreams. We can think about what it would feel like for our dreams to come true. This is essentially visualization, but adding a sprinkle of romanticization gives it a different depth.

1. Have something in mind you want to romanticize about. It could be an object (like a new car or house), a milestone (like a new job), or a person (like a new partner or friend). You

could also romanticize someone you already know; perhaps you would like to reignite the fire in a romantic relationship.

2. In your sacred space, dress two green candles with diluted rose geranium essential oil. As you light them, let your romanticization come to the forefront of your mind.

3. On a green piece of paper, write down what dream you are romanticizing. Then sprinkle lots of brown sugar on top of the paper.

4. Fold the piece of paper like an envelope, ensuring the sugar does not fall out. Place it in front of the candles.

5. On your censer, light a charcoal tablet and add three myrrh tears. Let this spiritual essence cleanse you. Allow it to penetrate your heart and engage the romantic side of your personality.

6. Sit down and start meditating. Go to that place within that makes you feel warm inside, the place where dreams within your subconscious mind come true.

7. Feel your desire for the dream you are romanticizing. Think about why you need it in your life. Embrace it fully.

8. Once the candles consume, pick up your little green envelope. Place it in a mailing envelope. Address it to yourself and drop it in the mail.

9. Once your envelope is delivered by the postal service, place the green envelope you made under your pillow and sleep on it every night. Soon, the dream you romanticized will come to be.

A SPELL FOR HOPE

Hope is the essence of humanity. In hard times, hope is what keeps us going. But oftentimes, hope is silenced by our logic, just like dreams and intuition are. Deep down, we dismiss feelings of hope when we need them most. We all need hope; we need to know things will get better. Here is a spell to keep hope in your heart.

1. Go to your sacred space. Light a charcoal tablet and on it burn myrrh, frankincense, and sage together. Let the smoke engulf you.

2. Wave a garnet crystal and a malachite crystal over this sacred smoke. As you do, visualize your hope becoming stronger. Remind yourself that the minute you lose hope in a situation or a relationship, you are giving up. Say:

Hope is an appendage I cannot live without

3. Place the crystals in a small, green drawstring bag. Add lavender flowers. Say:

Hope is within me, and I will never let it go

4. Every time you carry this little bag with you, hope is walking by your side.

A Spell to be Romantically Noticed

1. Draw a warm bath. As the tub is filling, dress a green and pink candle with diluted lavender essential oil. Light the candles, visualizing people noticing you everywhere you go.

2. Once the bathwater is ready, add fresh coriander, seven cherry pits from cherries you consumed, a cup of barley sugar, a few drops of rose geranium essential oil, and, lastly, the petals of a red rose.

3. Submerge yourself in the bath, visualizing yourself as a loving person. See yourself being noticed, either by someone you know or by someone you are yet to meet. The key to being noticed is to feel good about who you really are. Spend some time listing the things you love about yourself.

4. Stay in the bath for about twenty minutes. Make sure to get your hair wet. Get out of the bathwater without rinsing off. (Do not rinse off the spell for at least a day.) Pat yourself dry to seal the energy within you.

5. Drain the water and dispose of anything left in the tub.

6
Blue and Indigo

Blue is an incredibly soothing color. When we're angry and need to cool off, or when we are filled with sorrow, many people find comfort near the water. Blue brings tranquility and peace to the soul.

Blue is also the color of communication and understanding. It encourages you to speak your mind, especially when you need the courage to speak up against injustice, whether it is against others or yourself.

Everyday Uses of Blue

Blue is a color of peace and protection. It calms emotions and counteracts negative forces. Wear blue clothing to stabilize the physical body when you are sick, or when you are recovering from illness. If you suffer from anger issues, wear blue or light a blue candle to soothe irritation and bring peace to the soul.

Too much blue can make us overreact and speak negatively to others. Not enough blue can make us timid, too shy to speak our minds, and resistant to change.

BLUE COLOR MAGIC

I love to use the color blue in my magic—it's the keeper of the peace! Not only does it calm and even banish anger, it also manifests tranquility in the home. It's the color I use in most of my protection spells, as it pacifies others' initial intent so you don't get the brunt of it. Use blue while meditating and when reflecting on emotional reactions.

TO CALM THE ANGER WITHIN

Do you know a person who is angry with the world? Or maybe they deal with anger issues. To calm the anger within, carve their name into a blue candle and light it. As the wax melts away, so too will their anger.

For Everyday Peace

Whenever you want your home to feel peaceful, burn a white candle and a blue candle. If you have a chaotic life, lighting blue and white candles when you get home can help you relax.

For Faithful Partners

To keep your partner happy in all aspects of your relationship, light a green candle and a blue candle, preferably on Wednesday.

For Harmony

Light a blue candle first thing in the morning to bring harmony to your day. If you've had a bad day, burn blue candles to keep the stressors at bay. I always burn a blue candle on my bad days to keep the peace within.

To Heal Friendships

To heal a friendship or to make amends, light a white candle and a blue candle on a Wednesday.

For Health and Well-Being

For a loved one's health needs, light a white and a blue candle and visualize the healing that is needed.

To Move on After an Emotional Breakup

After the breakup of a relationship, light a blue candle and a yellow candle. The flames of these candles will help you move on. Alternatively, you could light them and say the name of a person who needs help moving on.

To Reveal Your Inner Self

On a Monday night, burn a pink and a blue candle. This will bring the real you to the surface, and it will encourage others to see you and accept you for who you are.

Jupiter

Attributes: Money, Legal Aid,
Personal Goals and Aspirations

Jupiter is a source of hope when there is none in sight. This is one planet that will not turn its back on you. On the contrary, it will stay by your side and look after your best interests. Writers, poets, and artists can call on Jupiter when they need inspiration; Jupiter always encourages creativity and visualizing your dreams. It wants us to overcome our daily challenges, especially challenges that are spiritual in nature.

This planet is smart and intuitive. Jupiter has a warm and friendly energy. When you need a father figure who is easy to talk to but also has a firm hand, Jupiter is the planet to invoke. Jupiter has a way of making you see the error of your ways diplomatically; it helps us understand why we do the things we do.

Common traits of this planet are moving forward with optimism as well as acquiring financial stability and abundance. Jupiter loves to share its fortune.

Day of the Week: Thursday

Thursday is a great day to do money spells and spells for financial stability. When we do money magic on Thursdays, we can attract money we never dreamed was within reach. Thursday is also a good day to pursue business ventures, like signing a contract, finalizing a divorce, or handling any type of personal settlements.

This day of the week cements ideas on paper. If there are documents that need to be signed for a favorable outcome, this is the day to do it. If you have to go to court, Thursday is the perfect day—

and if you have a clear head and Jupiter on your side, there is good chance your case will be heard favorably.

BLUE SPELLS WITH JUPITER ON THURSDAYS

Jupiter encourages us to keep fighting for our dreams and reminds us that we can achieve anything we set our mind to. It is a strong, just planet.

A SPELL FOR INJUSTICE

Being wronged or accused of something we haven't done can destroy our reputation. Justice sometimes turns into injustice in the blink of an eye, and not just on a personal level. If you feel you have been wronged and want the truth to shine, do this spell on a Thursday.

1. Go to your sacred space and dress three blue candles with olive oil.

2. In a small bowl, place a teaspoon of black pepper and a teaspoon of cumin powder. Mix these truth-telling spices and herbs together. As you do, think of the truth you want to surface.

3. Press the mixture onto each of the candles, then light them. As you do, say:

Your mouth will tingle until the truth is told

4. Now, on a piece of blue paper, write the name of the person that has committed the injustice. (If you don't know their name, write *To the one I seek justice from*.) Below that, write:

I forgive you for the past, but accountable for your actions you shall be

5. Sprinkle salt and pepper on the piece of paper.

6. Fold the piece of paper as many times as you can and place it between the candles until they have burned themselves out.

7. Keep this bundle somewhere safe until the truth is told. Then and only then can you throw it in the bin.

A Spell for Success

Success comes in many shapes and sizes: there is financial success, artistic success, successful parenting, successful employment, etc. There are many different ways to measure success as well. This spell is flexible and can be done for all different types of success.

1. In a small bowl, add a teaspoon of uncooked rice and a teaspoon of olive oil. Mix together until you have a paste.

2. Go to your sacred space and dress two blue and one orange candle with this mixture. Make sure to press the rice into the candle so it doesn't slide down straight away.

3. Light a charcoal tablet. Once done, place dry basil leaves on top. Let the smoke engulf the candles, then light them while thinking of the success you are wishing for.

4. On a piece of blue paper, write down what kind of success you are seeking. Write this with a blue feather. Ideally, you would use a blue quill, but if you cannot find one, you can make your own using a blue feather.

5. Place the paper in the middle of the candles. Let the candles consume.

6. Once the candles have burned out, sprinkle nutmeg powder on top of the piece of paper.

7. Burn the paper using matches or a lighter. Make sure to burn it safely; I recommend using a cast-iron pan or other firesafe object.

8. Take the paper's ashes and scatter them in a place that correlates with the success you are seeking. As you do so, say:

> **Hear my beating heart**
> **The success I need, I wish it to be**
> **Unselfish it is and will be**

9. Spend some time meditating and visualizing your success.

A Spell to Stop a Bully

Being bullied is one of the most destructive ways to weaken a person's emotional well-being. It is an intimidation spell that weakens the etheric field and makes it more susceptible to negative energy. A bully is a type of negative energy that is constantly poking their victim, even if they never touch the person. Their thoughts and actions are negative and dark. When you need to stop a bully, either for yourself or another, try this spell.

1. In your sacred space, dress two black candles and two blue candles with olive oil while thinking of the bully.

2. On a blue piece of paper, write the name of the bully. Then jot down a bulleted list of all the things you want the bully to stop doing to you or someone else.

3. Place the piece of paper in the middle of the four candles. Light the black candles first. As you do, say:

The constant bullying you inflict
upon me is known to the Universe
Soon you'll be facing trial and
answering to the wrongdoings you've
done to me and others like me

Light the blue candles, saying:

Leave me alone, and the others you've hurt
Go in peace
I will always be a better person than you will ever be
For the good of all, leave me in peace

4. Sprinkle salt on the blue piece of paper, and fold the paper to keep it in place.

5. With a blue ribbon, tie three knots around the paper. As you do, say:

You will never harm anyone again

6. Bury this bundle on the right side of your house. Only dig it up after you see results in front of your eyes. If the bullying starts again, repeat this spell as many times as it takes for the bully to get a universal message.

A SPELL FOR LEGAL AID

Finding the right person to represent you in a legal matter is harder than you might think. You might be wondering if this person is representing you because they are really interested in supporting you, or if they're just taking your case for the money. This spell can help you find legal aid with pure intentions.

1. On a Thursday at sunrise, go to your backyard or balcony. In each of your hands, place a diluted drop of lavender essential oil. Gently spread the oil on the palms of your hands until it's evenly distributed.

2. To keep the energy of the lavender oil in your hands, clasp them together in front of you. Visualize the traits of the legal aid you wish to find, and think about the drive they will need to help your case reach a positive outcome.

3. Then, gently rub the palms of your hands together and start building energy. Visualize a blue energy sphere forming.

While you are building this energy, think of the legal aid you need.

4. When you feel the sphere in your hands become the size of a baseball, direct your thoughts into the energy sphere like a flash of lightning, then let the sphere float into the sky. As the sphere floats away, believe that your message will reach the right person.

5. Twenty-four hours later, start looking for your legal aid. You will find the right person for the job.

Indigo

The color indigo is vibrant, with deep purple undertones. It's electric in some color blends, but it is a smooth, gentle, loving color that stands by tradition. In the fashion industry, indigo is a formal color, often seen on bridesmaids dresses, mother of the bride dresses, high school prom dresses, and on men's dress shirts, ties, and suits. This tells us that indigo is not only stylish, but festive at the same time.

Indigo represents our spiritual self, our spiritual values, and the innate wisdom in each of us. When we wear indigo, it helps us feel love for ourself and for others. In meditation, indigo takes us to our highest self. It helps us tune in to its messages while appreciating how long it took to hear them. Indigo aids communication with those not of this world.

This color is impartial and sees both sides of the story. Due to its neutrality in all things, it alleviates feelings of sadness and brings a cease-fire to tormented souls seeking peace of mind.

Everyday Uses of Indigo

Indigo is useful when working with the laws of karma. Use a lapis lazuli crystal when meditating or performing psychic work, or when you want to communicate your needs to the Universe. Be mindful of the fact that too much indigo can make you doubt your beliefs and intuition.

INDIGO COLOR MAGIC

I like to use indigo in spells when I want to set things right. It's also great for working with karmic situations because it brings a sense of justice to any situation. This is a great color to work with for peace of mind. Indigo also enhances communication with your spiritual guides.

A Spell to Find the Truth

1. Go to your sacred space, light a charcoal tablet, and place the shells of three sunflower seeds on top. Keep adding shells as they consume. Let this smoke engulf your space.

2. Dress an indigo candle with olive oil while thinking about the truth you need to hear.

3. Light the candle, saying:

Let the truth come forth
Until it is known to those who need to hear it the most

4. Sit back and wait. The truth will be heard.

For New Employment Jitters

Carry an indigo handkerchief with you on your first day at a new job. It will soothe the jitters so you can relax in your new environment.

7
Purple

*Attributes: Meditation, Relaxation,
Acceptance, Restful Sleep*

Purple initiates karmic relationships, so this color is excellent for meditation and any psychic work you may want to undertake. I find it easier to get in touch with my spiritual guides when working with purple; it opens doors to the spiritual realm. Purple is the color of our higher self, and it's the color of the third eye chakra. The third eye chakra communicates with everything we can't feel or see. Not only is purple intuitive, it calms the mind when we feel tormented or saddened by events beyond our control. It can also soothe physical aches and pains.

Everyday Uses of Purple

Wrap a purple shawl around you to feel immediate peace and comfort. A lit purple candle is great to meditate with because this color can be used to open your third eye chakra and helps you be more in tune with your intuition and psychic abilities.

Too much purple can cause headaches, symptoms of depression, an inability to envision the future, and a lack of compassion. Not enough purple can keep you from being in the moment and leads to frustration when you can't figure things out.

PURPLE COLOR MAGIC

Purple is a mixture of red and blue, which are two of the most powerful colors. Red represents passion and strength, while blue calms and soothes the mind, body, and spirit. When you think about it, purple can lend its magic to almost any situation. This is why purple is such a magnificent color to work with.

To Stop Disagreement

To stop family and friends from disagreeing, keep fresh gardenias and lavender around. If you are gathering somewhere other than your home, bring a bouquet of gardenias and lavender with you.

TO UNWIND

Light purple candles to relax after a hard day at work, or to release the tension after a difficult conversation with loved ones.

A SPELL FOR RELAXATION

Making time for relaxation is crucial for well-being, but many of us are so busy we do not make time to relax. If you struggle to find peace after a long day, try this easy spell.

1. In your sacred space, dress a blue candle and a purple candle with diluted lavender essential oil.

2. Turn on soft, relaxing music. Choose something that makes you feel calm. This may be nature sounds, a spa playlist, or an acoustic album.

3. Light the candles, then sit or lie down nearby. If you have a chair or cushion in your sacred space, this is the perfect time to use it. If not, bring a blanket or pillow(s) into your sacred space. Get as comfortable as possible.

4. Close your eyes and visualize the candles' flames and the peace they bring to your space. Think of everything that is good in the world and in your life. Continue thinking positive thoughts until you find peace within yourself.

5. When the candles have consumed, turn off the music and go about the rest of your day.

A SPELL TO ENHANCE MEDITATION

If you are new to meditation or struggle to quiet your mind, purple is an excellent color to work with. Use this spell when you want to access a deeper meditative state.

1. In your sacred space, dress two purple candles with diluted lavender essential oil.

2. Set an amethyst crystal in front of the candles, then light them.

3. Get into your favorite meditating position. Once you're comfortable, pick up the amethyst crystal and hold it in your right hand. Feel its vibration go through you. Close your eyes and start your meditation.

4. Meditate for as long as you feel called to do so, holding the crystal in your right hand the entire time.

5. Let the candles consume. Leave the amethyst crystal in your sacred space for your next meditation experience.

A Spell to Connect to a Spiritual Guide

Getting in touch with spiritual guides is extremely easy for some people, but for others, it can be quite challenging. Rest assured, once the connection is made, it will be easier the next time around. Try this spell when you want to connect to one of your guides.

1. Fill a glass with tap water and place it in your sacred space.

2. Dress a white, a purple, and a pink candle with olive oil. As you do, visualize the connection you wish to make with your guides. Once done, line them up in a straight line and light them.

3. Place the glass of water in front of the candles. Think of the glass of water as your mind, clear as light. Keep looking at the glass and enter a light meditative state.

4. Start visualizing what you think your guide looks like. See your guide as clearly as if they were standing right in front of you. Trust your intuition.

5. When you can see your guide, tell them the reason you want to make a connection. If help is needed, don't be shy—ask for it! Your guides want to be of assistance. Also ask your guides for a sign that they heard you. You will receive one, but it may not be right then; sometimes it takes days for you to get your answer.

6. Let the candles burn themselves out. Toss the water you used into your garden or a potted plant.

Lilac

Like all shades of purple, lilac is a blend of red and blue. When you add white to these two colors, the color lilac comes into existence. I tend to associate the color lilac with grandmothers: all nice and warm, not to mention cuddly! Even the smell of lilacs may take some of us back to a time we felt safe and loved in someone's arms.

LILAC COLOR MAGIC

This color brings serenity into the world. Lilac helps us understand the balance of life and reflect on lessons learned. It holds knowledge of times gone by and knowledge of all that is yet to come. Lilac likes uncharted ground, and it brings bravery to the forefront. This color helps you see logic in times of uncertainty; it is welcoming and nurturing.

A Spell for Peace of Mind

1. In your sacred space, dress two lilac candles with diluted lilac essential oil. As you do this, visualize yourself in a wooded area, then light the candles.

2. Feel the peace the woods bring. Hear the birds' gentle chirps and the light wind whispering through the trees. Visualize the torment within leaving your mind, body, and soul.

3. Let the flicker of the candles' flames bring you the peace you seek. Let the candles consume to the end.

A Spell to Accept the Past

1. Dress yourself in all lilac. If you are unable to do so, find a lilac wrap (or sarong or large scarf) and place it around you while wearing white undergarments.

2. Go outside and find a plush patch of grass. With your right foot, make a circle around you and stand in the middle.

3. Dig your heels into the ground and visualize a lilac light around you. Let the earth ground you. Feel the energy it offers. Feel the peace and acceptance it brings to your heart and soul.

4. Spread your arms out and let go of your past, your deepest hurts and sorrows. Visualize those hurts and sorrows penetrating the earth beneath you.

5. Once finished, get cold water and pour it where you stood. All past hurts will stay frozen and buried forevermore.

A SPELL TO HEAL A RELATIONSHIP

Before beginning, think about which relationship in your life you would like to heal. Then, find a photo taken when happy times existed between you and the other person. This may be a partner, sibling, parent, or former friend. You will need this photo to begin the spell.

1. Place the photo you have selected in your sacred space.

2. In your mortar and pestle, place four or five cooking cloves. Grind them into powder. As you do this, keep in mind what you want to heal within the relationship. Once this is done, dust the powder over the photo, still thinking about the healing you want to occur.

3. Dress two lilac candles and one green candle with olive oil, then place the candles around the photo in a triangular shape.

Set the green candle near the top of the photo, representing the tip of the triangle, and the two lilac candles at the bottom.

4. Light the green candle first, and as you do, visualize yourself and the person in question healing any hurts or misjudgments that have occurred.

5. Next, light the lilac candles. As you light the first candle, visualize things as they once were. When you light the second lilac candle, visualize the healing that is needed to return the relationship to the way it once was.

6. Let the candles burn themselves out. Once they have consumed, roll up the picture so that the clove dust remains inside. Keep the photo in a treasured place, and you'll notice that over time, the healing needed will manifest.

A Spell to Let Go of the Past

1. On a green piece of paper, write down what you want to let go of. Do this in black ink. Be as detailed as you'd like.

2. Dress a black candle with jojoba oil. As you do, think of how the past is hindering the future, then light the candle.

3. Dress a green candle and a lilac candle with olive oil. While you do, visualize healing the past, then light the candles. Place all the candles on top of your green piece of paper.

4. In a diffuser, add a few drops of lilac essential oil. Let this essence heal your heart.

5. Let your candles consume. Once they have burned out, take the piece of paper outside. In a controlled, fireproof environment, set the paper on fire.

6. When there are only ashes left, let them be taken by nature's gentle breeze. As the ashes blow away, let your past be whisked away as well.

Lavender

Lavender represents peace and harmony. It also has a sense of grace and respect. It can keep you calm in stressful situations, especially if the situation has to do with your family or things outside your control.

Lavender can provide relief for chronic conditions and issues, especially those that are mental in nature. Because lavender helps your mind find peace, use it to settle unresolved emotions and to keep anxiety within peaceful parameters.

LAVENDER COLOR MAGIC

This is the color of rest and sleep. It brings peace to the day's stressors. Lavender facilitates love entering your life, not only from outside forces, but also from within.

TO SOOTHE SICKNESS

To aid symptoms of illness, give the person who is ill an amethyst crystal and a warm, heartfelt hug.

FOR A BETTER NIGHT'S SLEEP

Put white and lavender sheets on your bed. Paint one of the walls in your bedroom lavender, or find a piece of artwork with lavender tones and hang it near your bed. Sheer lavender curtains will enhance the restful ambience.

A SPELL TO HEAL A TRAUMATIC MEMORY

1. In your sacred space, dress two white candles and one lavender candle with diluted lavender essential oil.

2. As you light the candles, think of a traumatic event from your past that you wish to heal. If needed, take a moment to ground yourself in your current surroundings before continuing.

3. On a white piece of paper, write down what you wish to let go or come to terms with. Use a green pen or pencil. Write as much or as little as you'd like. Once you're finished, place the piece of paper in your sacred space.

4. Light a charcoal tablet and place a few sage leaves on top. Let the smoke engulf you. Breathe in this healing smoke. Feel it cleansing you and taking away all that you don't want to carry any longer.

5. Take your piece of paper and, bit by bit, tear it into tiny pieces. Place these pieces on the charcoal tablet a few at a time, continuing to add sage to the mix in small amounts. While the tablet burns, visualize traumatic memories leaving your heart and soul.

A SPELL TO CONNECT TO YOUR INNER SANCTUM

Do you seem to have a never-ending to-do list? If so, you're not alone. Most of us are exhausted, yet we do not allow ourselves time to relax. We let our busyness get in the way of our well-being.

You must give yourself permission to be pampered and to rest and recharge. Prioritize connecting to your inner sanctum, that sacred place that is yours and yours alone. Set aside a half an hour for yourself. You may have all sorts of excuses, but the only thing I can say (and I say this to myself): *make the time.*

1. Dress two lavender candles with diluted lavender essential oil. Take them to your bathroom along with lavender essential oil, lavender food coloring, a few bundles of lavender flowers, and two white roses.

2. Start preparing your bath. As the bathtub fills, light your candles, then turn off the bathroom lights.

3. Once your bathtub has finished filling, add the following to the water: three drops of lavender essential oil, two drops of the food coloring, and the bundle of lavender flowers. Then pluck the petals off the white roses and sprinkle the petals into the water. Finally, add a cup of magnesium flakes.

4. Ask everyone in the household to respect your privacy for at least a half an hour. Turn on some soothing music, sink into the warm water, and enjoy this much-needed relaxing time.

5. Once you're done in the bath, pat yourself dry to seal the energy within.

A SPELL FOR RESTFUL SLEEP

1. Fill a glass with water, then add only the white of an egg. Observe the different shapes forming in the water and how they gently sway when you move the glass. As you stare into the glass, visualize getting a good night's sleep.

2. Place the glass under your bed, below where your pillow is. If you can't put it under the bed, put it on your bedside table.

3. Once this is accomplished, light an unscented purple pillar candle. If you can't find an unscented purple candle, use one that is scented with lavender essential oil. If using an unscented candle, burn lavender essential oil in a diffuser.

4. Let the candle burn for at least half an hour. If using a diffuser, let it run for thirty minutes. Then snuff the candle and get in bed.

5. Consider this candle and lavender scent to be a nightly ritual. Repeat steps 1 through 4 the following night. Make sure to use a fresh egg white in fresh water; the one from the night before should be flushed down the toilet.

6. Do this for three straight nights, then repeat the process as needed.

A SPELL FOR A HARMONY BOWL

Think about which room of your house is most frequently occupied by the people you live with. If you live alone, think about which room you spend the most time in. Perform this spell in that room to establish harmony in the home.

1. Place an unscented lavender pillar candle in a candleholder. Set this in a shallow decorative bowl, preferably lavender in color.

2. Around the candle, place a few oranges. Sprinkle cumin seeds. Add a few Brazilian nuts to the mix, as well as a few cinnamon sticks and bay leaves. Spend as much time arranging the items as you'd like. No matter what, it will be stunning when finished.

3. Think of the harmony you wish to achieve. You may want to direct this energy to a specific person, or to the whole group, depending on the household's dynamics. If you live alone, visualize harmony for yourself and your home.

4. Light the candle when you know you are home for the night. Before you go to bed each night, snuff the candle out.

5. When a new candle is needed, refresh all of the ingredients in the bowl. Replace the pillar candle. Sprinkle new seeds and add new oranges, nuts, cinnamon sticks, and bay leaves. Know that every time you light this candle, peace and harmony will fill your home.

8

Pink

Pink is the color of love, understanding, and everlasting friendship. It activates the love inside each one of us, and it helps us express that love to attract the one we seek.

Pink brings harmony, peace, and laughter; pacifies anger; and creates affection between all in the home. In magic, this color is used for love and self-love spells, to pacify anger or resentment, to investigate the past without being overwhelmed by old emotions, to soothe self-pitying thoughts, and to tap into the love within and jump-start the healing process.

Everyday Uses of Pink

As money is associated with green, love is with pink. Pink makes friends and helps keep them. It calls in love, especially the love within. When you work with the color pink, you express love more easily, and in turn, others will feel more comfortable showering you with their love. Light a pink candle to boost self-confidence. You can even wear pink in your hair to attract a new love interest.

Even though pink is a loving and healing color, too much pink can cause overconfidence and jealousy, and it may be hard to heal emotionally. On the other hand, too little pink may manifest as a lack of self-love and being closed off to loving relationships.

PINK COLOR MAGIC

I love working with the color pink. It is the color of relationships, both romantic and platonic, as well as the relationship we have with ourself.

TO ATTRACT A LOVER

Add a teaspoon of dry basil leaves and a rose quartz crystal to a small, pink drawstring bag to attract the kind of love you dream about.

To Find Love Within

When one of your friends is suffering from low self-esteem, print a picture of them and cover it with a pink silk cloth. This will help them feel the kind of love that only comes from deep within the soul.

To Fight Depression

When depression sets in, light a white candle and a pink candle to help ease its symptoms.

For a Successful Party

Whenever you have guests over, light white and pink candles to ensure a great gathering.

To Find Love

When you are ready to find that special someone, light a pink candle and a green candle each Friday. With time, someone for you to love will come along.

To Let Love In

When you feel you are lacking love within your life, whether it is romantic or platonic love, light pink and white candles.

TO DREAM OF YOUR FUTURE HOME

Visualizing your future home is great fun. Some people even dream about it! Light pink and blue candles a few hours before bedtime to reinforce your dreams by tenfold. You can also do this to boost dreams about your future in general.

TO DISCOURAGE FIGHTING

To reduce the number of arguments in the home, place a rose quartz crystal and a blue lace agate crystal in a white bowl. Set it in the room in your home that is most frequently occupied.

A LOVE NOTE

Write a love note on a pink piece of paper, then sprinkle half a teaspoon of crushed cardamom seeds on top. Let everything sit for a few minutes. When enough time has passed, go outside and blow the seeds in the direction of your lover for an ever-sweet reply.

If you are single, you can do this spell by writing a love note to the one you are in search of.

Planet: Venus

Attributes: Love, Friendship, Relationships

Venus's energy is similar to the moon's, but Venus is more lustful in some ways. Like the moon, Venus is loving and kind and exudes feminine energy. This planet rules relationships, not only the romantic ones but also the relationships we have with family, friends, and even coworkers.

This planet helps us appreciate what we already have, be it material or emotional. And no matter how you feel about your looks, Venus is there to tell you that you are beautiful. This planet helps us understand and value the unique beauty and grace we possess. However, be careful not to overdo it. Vanity is disliked by this planet—it goes against everything Venus represents. Not only does it dislike vanity, but Venus abhors unkindness to others.

Spicing up the love in your life and enjoying that special someone are Venus's fortes, and if you are single, rest assured this planet is looking for someone for you—but it doesn't hurt to nudge it a little with a spell.

Day of the Week: Friday

Venus embodies the essence of love, as does Friday, which is totally governed by romance and relationships. We tend to be happy on Fridays, and why wouldn't we be? For many of us, Friday is the end of the work week! That energy we feel is amplified by Venus. Bask in that joyful energy and utilize Fridays for self-love.

This is a good day to do magic aimed at discovering what the future has in store for you. Work on your relationships to make them more solid. This is the day to mend things with loved ones, perhaps even a brother, mother, or father whom you haven't been able to forgive for something they did in the past.

PINK SPELLS WITH VENUS ON FRIDAY

If you work with Venus and the color pink on Fridays, your relationships will thrive.

A SPELL FOR SELF-LOVE

We tend to worry more about our exterior than our interior. But for us to truly feel our best, we have to look in the mirror and like what we see. This is a challenge that many of us face on a daily basis, usually due to preconceived notions about how we should look or act. But we don't have to let society dictate how we feel about ourselves! This spell will help you find love from the inside out.

1. Cleanse a rose quartz crystal under cool running water, then place it inside a small glass bottle. Add water and a drop of pink food coloring, then close the lid.

2. In your sacred space, set the bottle on a pink cloth. Sprinkle the petals of three pink roses on the cloth. As you do, visualize the love you want to feel; imagine it blossoming inside you.

3. Wrap the pink cloth around the bottle, keeping the rose petals inside. Tie the cloth with a pink ribbon to keep it in place.

4. Take the wrapped bottle outside and place on the ground. Say:

Venus, shine on my bottle tonight
Fill it with the love I need within so I can be my true self
And not some magazine queen

5. First thing in the morning, bring the bottle in, unwrap it, and drink the water. (Be careful not to swallow the rose quartz crystal!)

6. Keep the rose quartz, bottle, and pink cloth should you want to use them again for another spell. Dispose of the pink rose petals in your yard.

A SPELL TO FIND ROMANTIC LOVE

If you are single, you know that dating is sometimes like trying to find the other shoe in a pair that has been missing for months. This spell can help.

1. Find two tiger's eye crystals that are about the same size and shape. Place them in a clear glass. Fill the glass with water and add a teaspoon of salt.

2. Leave the glass outside for three days and three nights.

3. When you are ready to conduct the spell, pour the glasses out and take the two crystals to your sacred space.

4. Dress two pink candles with diluted sandalwood essential oil. Light them while visualizing the romantic love you are seeking.

5. Get two pieces of paper. On one piece of paper, draw a shoe that you would wear. On the other piece of paper, draw a shoe that you think the person you want to attract would wear.

6. On the drawing of your own shoe, write all the things you want in a romantic partner. Keep it simple and remember no one is perfect: you don't want to limit yourself to silly things, such as never leaving a towel on the floor.

7. On top of the drawings, sprinkle dill seeds. Then place a tiger's eye crystal on top of each drawing.

8. Fold the papers up separately, keeping the seeds and crystal inside, until you have two little bundles. Roll both inside a pink cloth and tie it closed with a pink ribbon. As you tie the ribbon, say:

I am looking for you as you are looking for me
Come and find me—I am a breath away

9. Let your breath fall on your romantic bundle, then place it outside somewhere it will be protected from the elements.

10. After three days, bring the bundle inside. Leave it in a romantic place that you hope to one day share with the love of your life.

A Spell to Strengthen Family Ties

Some families are close and band together when things get tough, but for whatever reason, your family may not be as close as you'd like. The family nucleus is so important to me—my friends know me, but my family knows me best. Use this spell to strengthen your family's bond.

1. In your sacred space, dress two pink candles and a blue candle with diluted jasmine essential oil. While you do this, think about the closeness you want your family to have.

2. Light the candles.

3. Arrange a few magnets near the candles. If there are three members of your family, you will need three or more magnets, depending on whom you want to bring closer together. The magnet size doesn't matter, but if there is a specific member you want to bring closer to the family nucleus, make sure to place their magnet in the middle of the rest of the magnets.

4. Light a charcoal tablet and add two pieces of frankincense resin. Let the smoke engulf your sacred space.

5. Hold the magnets in your hands and visualize the closeness you are hoping for. Quickly waft the magnets over the candles' flames and say:

Together as one we will be

6. Run the magnets over the smoke and say:

Quarrels forgiven and family to come together
As strong as these magnets
Venus, keep my family close
And repel those that disturb the family peace

7. Place the magnets in front of the candles. Place a bay leaf for each family member on top of the magnets.

8. Leave everything as is until the candles consume.

9. Once the candles have burned out, place the magnets and bay leaves in a pink drawstring bag. (You could also wrap them up in a pink cloth.) Keep it in a place the family gets together.

You can use this magnet spell for just about any relationship that needs to be drawn closer together. It works great for couples!

A SPELL TO HEAL A FRIENDSHIP AND MAKE THINGS RIGHT

Friendships are sacred, and when we know we've hurt one of our friends, it's painful for both parties. You may wish you had handled the situation differently, but what's done is done. When you are ready to make things right, use this spell to start healing the friendship.

1. Print out a picture of your friend and you together. Place it in your sacred space.

2. Dress three pink candles, a yellow candle, and a purple candle with diluted lavender essential oil. As you do this, think of the amends you wish to make and the things you wish you could take back.

3. Once the candles are dressed, make a circle with them. Alternate the colors so that the three pink candles aren't next to each other.

4. On the back of the photo, write: "I seek your forgiveness <u>(name)</u>." As you write this, say it out loud. Then place the photo in the middle of the candles.

5. Sprinkle yerba santa and fresh mint leaves on top of the photo. Say:

I am sorry I've hurt you

6. Now, light the candles. As you light each one, say:

I was wrong. I am better than that, forgive me
Open communication channels and accept my apology

7. Let the candles consume. Once they've burned out, roll up the photo while keeping the herbs inside. Wrap a yellow cloth around the photo. Leave it in a place where better times were had, and retrieve it only when the relationship has been repaired.

Remember that in order for the spell to work, you will need to open a channel of communication with your friend. This may mean sending them a text or a letter, or giving them a phone call. When you do reach out, do it on a Wednesday, which is the day of communication.

You can also do this spell for other types of relationships that need to be healed.

9
‘White

White is an impartial color. It is the empty canvas ready to take on whatever you draw, write, or manifest. White represents purity and harmony whenever it is utilized. It is a trusted color; it has no malice or ill intent. The color white can pacify negative workings and balance a spell without causing harm to the sender or receiver.

Because of this color's purifying energy, it is often used in healing rituals and spells. It is seen as a color of perfection, cleanliness, and freshness, but too much white can come off sterile and unfeeling.

White is the facilitator of communication with other realms and universal beings. Use it in meditation or when contacting your spiritual guides. This color contains the wisdom and comfort of the moon; it makes us feel safe and secure.

Everyday Uses of White

White is the color of the Universe, purity, unconditional love, and understanding. It is an excellent color to keep around sick and/or newborn babies because it's associated with tranquility and good health.

Too much white leads you to clinically analyze yourself and others. It makes a person see what they want to see, not what they *need* to see. Not having enough white in your life can make it harder for things to come to fruition, and the lack of harmony could cause depression.

WHITE COLOR MAGIC

Because the color white is peaceful and understanding, it helps us surrender things we have struggled to let go of. Use this color in spellwork for releasing. It is also a very protective color, so it can be a beneficial addition to any magical working.

For Answers

If you seek answers, white will provide them. Light a white candle and ask your guides for help.

When You Need to Know Why

If you feel wronged by the Universe, like everything is conspiring against you, set a bouquet of white flowers in your sacred space. Once you've left this offering, ask karma the reason(s) for the difficulties you are facing. You can also ask about the lessons you are supposed to be learning.

For Everyday Abundance

Place a citrine crystal in a bowl of uncooked rice and keep it in your kitchen. This will help ensure that your material needs are met.

To Dream of Your Future Love

Just one drop of jasmine essential oil on a white pillowcase will help you dream about your future partner. This oil will also help manifest the love you are seeking.

Spiritual Tips to Get Your Health Back

After being sick, regaining your health may be a slow process. It could take weeks or even months before you feel back to normal, especially if the illness was debilitating. I've included a list of spiritual tips to help you quickly regain your health after illness. These methods are tried and true—I've used them myself.

Within a five-year period, I had breast cancer twice. It was a difficult time filled with surgeries, radiation, chemotherapy, and a year's worth of infusions every twenty-one days, not to mention that I was going through treatment when the COVID-19 pandemic hit, so I was isolated.

During every single treatment, I did meditation and visualized the future full of health and happiness, but most importantly, I accepted what was in front of me, and it quickly was behind me. I embraced my treatments instead of fighting them. I knew I was going to get through it, and I did, and so will you. With whatever ails you. There is something to be learned from any illness: your attitude toward it is what gets you through.

Here are some ways to boost your health.

- Wear white, silver, or purple.

- Take healing baths. Add a few drops of lavender essential oil, three drops of purple food coloring, and a cup of magnesium flakes to bathwater.

- Maintain a healthy diet, and always eat at the table. Make sure your table has a white tablecloth.

- Drink herbal teas such as ginger.

- Stay positive by visualizing your spiritual and physical body healthy and well.

- Spend as much time outside as possible.

- Exercise or take a long walk in nature.

- Each day, get a hug from a loved one.

- Keep reminding yourself this will pass.

- Meditation or yoga are excellent tools for healing.

- Use your crystals. I recommend carrying clear quartz and amethyst. Clear quartz is great for physical and mental health, and amethyst brings peace and helps the body and heart heal from the trauma of illness.

- Burn incense in the home. I recommend frankincense, rosemary, and bergamot for spiritual health.

- Make Monday a healing day and seek guidance from the moon, your guides, and deities. Ask them to help you through this difficult time.

- Send positive energy to those who look after your health, such as your doctor.

- Make sure you have a community, whether that is family and friends or a support group; they will get you through the toughest times.

Planet: Moon

Attributes: Psychic Abilities, Health, Meditation, Communication with Guides, Divine Feminine

The moon influences Earth's tides and governs our emotions. When I think of the moon, I think of some of the most beautiful things in life, like beds of flowers and the blue waters of the ocean. The moon is compassionate, not to mention gentle and wise. When the moon is high in the sky, she reminds us to rest.

The moon is a healer; if the moon was personified, she would sit by your bedside, listen to your sadness, and cry with you, as she understands the pain you are going through. The moon holds those who are sick in her tender embrace, and she brings comfort to anyone burdened with unanswered questions. She soothes worries and turbulent emotions.

Day of the Week: Monday

Monday is the first day of the work week for many of us, and because of this, we may dread Mondays or dismiss the day's importance. Instead of begrudging the first day of the work week, I encourage you to embrace this spiritual day with open arms, and to welcome Monday and the moon into your heart.

Mondays are associated with the colors white and purple, and, of course, the moon. This is a day of discovery. On this day of the week, connect with universal forces and ask them to guide you and illuminate your future path. You may also find that you are more in tune with psychic work and meditation on Mondays.

Working with the Phases of the Moon

Instead of recommending working with the moon on Monday, I encourage you to work with the lunar phases. There are many resources that can help you determine what phase the moon is in on any given day.

Working with lunar phases is magical! The great thing about lunar phases is that you aren't limited to the days of the week. The moon does not change phases on particular days of the week; it varies month by month.

I have organized the spells in this chapter by moon phase. While the moon has several phases, the four I've focused on in this chapter are the full moon, waning moon, new moon, and waxing moon.

WHITE SPELLS FOR THE FULL MOON (GREAT POTENTIAL)

The full moon is bright and round. When the moon is full, it helps illuminate the dark—I find driving at night to be a much more pleasant experience during the full moon.

This is when the moon is at its most powerful. You can use the full moon's energy in all kinds of magic, be it positive, banishing, or whatever your needs may be. Many people consider the full moon to be a time of reflection and release.

A SPELL FOR EMOTIONAL HEALING

Soothing stressful emotions is one of the moon's best attributes, and we should take advantage of it. Try this spell during the full moon.

1. The day after the full moon, dress in all white, including your undergarments. Affix a fresh white flower in your hair. Stand in your backyard or visit a park when the moon is out and bright. Take with you five tealight candles, a clear quartz crystal, and half a cup of poppy seeds.

2. Place the tealights on the ground in a circle. Make sure it is wide enough that you can sit inside the circle without it being a fire hazard.

3. Light the tealights. As you light each one, think of the emotions you want to heal.

4. Sit cross-legged in the middle of the tealights, placing the clear quartz crystal on the ground in front of you. Close your eyes and feel united with the earth below you and moon above you. Say:

**I seek emotional well-being from
my troubled emotional life**

5. Place both hands on the ground. Dig your fingers into the soil and visualize every pain, loss, or misfortune that you carry leaving through your fingers and being absorbed by nature and the light of the moon.

6. Sprinkle the poppy seeds around you. As you do, say:

**Absorb my emotional unsettlement
May it not carry to another lifetime
But finish with this one**

7. Stay seated and look at the moon. Know that you will wake up in the morning feeling a lot better, with strengthened emotional well-being.

A SPELL FOR GENERAL HEALING

I like to use oaks in healing spells. This spell combines the power of the oak with the magic of the color white.

1. Using a sewing pin, write your general health wish on top of an acorn. I know this is difficult to do, so take your time. As you carve, keep your message on your mind.

2. Once finished, wrap white ribbon around your acorn and secure with a knot. Include a loop in the ribbon so it can be hanged.

3. Find an oak tree, preferably one on your property. Ask the mighty oak for permission to hang your little healing bundle on one of its branches. Say:

Mighty oak, I need your
strength to help me get well
May I hang this acorn from your
branches for only three days?

4. Await a response from the mighty oak. You will know permission has been granted if a breeze comes your way, a leaf falls, or your heart tells you you have permission.

5. Once you have permission, hang your bundle on one of the tree's branches. Say:

Thank you, I will be back in three days

6. For the next three days, whenever your spell crosses your mind, visualize your acorn being infused with the oak's energy and health.

7. On the third day, retrieve your bundle and say:

Thank you, mighty oak
Your strength is needed to be healthy and well again

8. Keep the acorn close to your chest. Feel it giving you the strength you need to stay healthy and well. When needed, repeat the process with a new acorn.

WHITE SPELLS FOR THE WANING MOON (REWORKING OR REMOVING)

Between the full moon and the new moon, the moon is waning. This is when the moon appears to decrease in size.

Since the moon appears to be getting smaller during the waning moon, this is a good time to work against negative forces. Banish unwanted energies, eliminate self-doubt, and quiet your noisy neighbor or nagging boss.

SPIRITUAL TIPS FOR BANISHING NEGATIVE ENERGY

When the moon starts to shrink in size, let go of things that have hurt you. There is not always a need for complicated spells; the simplest things can manifest the same outcome during this phase of the moon.

When banishing negative energy, here are some things to keep in mind: Anything you write, burn, or bury works wonders for the soul. Anything you freeze stops energy in its tracks. Anything you rip or cut slashes it. Anything you pop shreds it.

- When you want to let something go, I recommend writing it down. Bury the piece of paper if you never want to go through something like that again, or burn it if you want to destroy the memory.

- If someone has been working against you and you want to stop them, write their name on a piece of paper. Place the piece of paper in a freezer-safe glass or container, then fill it with water. Once done, stick it in the freezer. As the water freezes, so will the person's negative actions. This is a harmless way to stop negative people in their tracks. I've known people who had dozens of these glasses in their freezer at a time! Please, if the problem ends, unfreeze the piece of paper and dispose of it. It's not a good idea to keep someone frozen forever. If you unfreeze the paper and then notice negativity starting up again, by all means repeat the spell.

- Balloons are assets to the magical world, but we often forget to utilize them. Blow into a white balloon until it is half full, then grab a marker. Write what you want to let go of on the balloon, then finish blowing it up and knot the bottom. Take it outside and pop it with a pin.

- You can always come up with your own ways to let go of emotional baggage. Be creative! With that being said, don't burn, bury, freeze, or pop anything with the intent of causing harm to others.

A SPELL FOR A FRIENDLIER NEIGHBORHOOD

Some of us have amazing neighbors: they are always willing to feed the dog, watch the house when you're on holiday, or pick you up from the mechanic. Unfortunately, not all neighbors are like that—some neighbors are the total opposite. Use this spell when you want to build a stronger relationship with one of your neighbors.

1. On Google Earth, find the street your home is on. Make sure your home is in frame, as well as your neighbor's home. Print the image in color, then head off to your sacred space.

2. Get two white candles. Write your neighbor's address (house number and street name) on one of the candles with a pin. On the other candle, write your address, using the same pin. As you are doing this, keep in mind the changes you would like to see from your neighbor, changes that will make both of your lives easier.

3. Dress the candles with olive oil.

4. On your printed street map, place your candle on top of your home and your neighbor's candle on top of theirs, visualizing what cycles you want to end. Light the candles while saying:

Let us be neighborly and not enemies

5. Let the candles consume to the end. Once they've burned out, roll up the street map and bury it in your backyard. All that happened between you and your neighbor is now in the past; change will come around.

WHITE SPELLS FOR THE NEW MOON (BEGINNINGS)

The new moon is not visible in the sky. This is because of the angle between the sun and the moon during this lunar phase. But while the new moon may be hidden from us, it is still there, and this is one of the best times to do magic.

New moons are excellent for manifesting. Focus on new beginnings: this could be a new relationship, a career change, or the decision to go back to school. During the new moon, focus on the things you've always wanted, especially those that were previously out of reach. Use this lunar phase to make your wishes come true.

A SPELL FOR A SECRET WISH

Some people have a difficult time believing in their manifestations, but it's important to focus on hope, not doubt. Change often presents itself when we least expect it. Use this spell to manifest one of your deepest wishes. Choose a wish that you feel strongly about. This may be something you've never shared with anyone before—that's okay. Dream big! Always remember, no wish is too far-fetched.

1. Go to your sacred space. Dress a white candle and a silver candle with diluted jasmine essential oil.

2. On your censer, light a charcoal tablet. Place sage leaves on top. Let the smoke engulf you while you visualize your deepest desire.

3. Light the candles with your wish in mind. Say:

   Wishes do come true, if from the heart they are felt

4. Around the candles, create a circle made of walnuts. In the middle of the candles, place a rose quartz crystal. During this process, think about your wish as if it was already reality.

5. After ten minutes, snuff the candles.

6. Light the candles for ten minutes every day for seven days.

7. On the seventh day, let the candles consume right to the end. Take the walnuts and the rose quartz crystal into your front yard. (If you do not have a front yard, you could do this at a park or in a wooded area.) Lay the walnuts and the crystal on the lawn, making a circle, and say:

Here I leave a token for the wish made in secrecy
Dear lady, take it and grant it and I will hold it dearly

8. Leave the walnuts and the crystal on the grass. Don't tell anyone your wish; just wait patiently for it to manifest.

A SPELL FOR ABUNDANCE

There are different types of abundance: health, happiness, financial, and even protective. The good thing about this spell is that it doesn't limit you to just one type of abundance; it is always good to be open-minded when visualizing abundance, as you don't want to miss out on any prosperity the moon has to share.

1. Dress three silver candles with a mixture of diluted lavender essential oil and basil essential oil. As you dress your candles, visualize abundance nourishing you from the inside out, saying:

**I feel the love within me
I feel health brightening my cheeks
Happiness filling my heart
And protection with every step I take**

2. Light the candles and say:

**Fill any absence with the abundance I need
Make it so**

3. Let the candles consume. Get ready for abundance to rain down upon you!

White Spells for the Waxing Moon (Building)

Between the new moon and the full moon, the moon is waxing. This means it appears to be growing in size. As the moon grows into its full potential, so can you!

This is a good time to do spellwork that focuses on enhancing what you have while continuing to work toward your goals. If you would like to see improvement in your health or even wealth, work with the waxing moon.

WHEN YOU NEED MONEY

Money makes the world go 'round, but it shouldn't be a priority over health, love, and happiness. With that being said, there are times when our wallets could use a little gold dusting. Below are a few things you can do during the waxing moon to boost your finances:

- Anoint your front door with basil essential oil. You could also use jasmine essential oil.

- Pour sesame seeds into a bowl and visualize each seed as a dollar bill.

- Green is the color of growth, so wear lots of it.

- Red jasper and citrine crystals bring about financial security.

- Walk past a bank and visualize all its money going into your wallet.

- Eat lots of almonds. Each time you eat an almond, visualize this little nut bringing money to your front door. (You can do this with any nut—they are all good for money magic.)

- Place a bunch of fresh basil in a vase. Replace it on Sundays for best results.

- Having a cup of mint tea is not only delicious, but it can invite riches into your world.

- Cloves and cinnamon are a must. Burn them on your censer as many times a day as you can.

A SPELL TO BE VALUED AT WORK

Sometimes our bosses take us for granted. Your boss might cancel a meeting last minute, forget to give you credit for an idea, or expect you to do something at a moment's notice without even asking if you have capacity. If you feel that your work goes unnoticed in your place of employment, let's change that! This spell will make you feel appreciated, valued, and respected in the workplace.

1. Set a white candle and two purple candles in your sacred space.

2. In a bowl, shred some fresh ginger, then place it in your mortar and pestle. Add three drops of lemon essential oil, then mix together.

3. Start to dress your candles with this mixture. As you do, think about how you would like to be noticed. If you only have one boss, then visualize your boss noticing all the special things

you do around the office. Imagine them thanking you for the hard work you do. Say:

Noticed and respected I shall be
From this day forward

4. Place the white candle in the middle of the two purple ones. Light the purple candles first, then the white, while saying:

Valued I shall be
A "thank you" and a "please" from you to me
Will be greatly appreciated

5. Let the candles burn to the end. Hopefully you have a little wax leftover. While the leftover wax is still warm, roll it into a ball. Go outside and throw this ball in the direction of your workplace. From now on, your boss will know you are worth every penny, and they will treat you with more respect.

10
Brown

Brown is not one of the brightest colors. It's often perceived as a gloomy, sullen color and is typically worn during winter months. It's more of a structural color; think of brown paints and furnishings.

I like to think brown possesses the strength of a tree trunk. This color has a sturdiness unlike any other, but it remains true to the tender personality it possesses. And of course brown is grounded like tree roots, embedded deep within the earth.

Unfortunately, brown can also be unpredictable and change its structure in a matter of seconds. Think about nature and the way fire, flooding, washouts, tornados, hurricanes, earthquakes, and tsunamis can change our surroundings in the blink of an eye. This makes the color brown something of a chameleon, always changing and hard to work with on a spiritual level. But brown is also adaptable—cunning, even— due to its unpredictability.

Everyday Uses of Brown

A cup of hot chocolate can bring peace and comfort on a cold, rainy day. I am partial to a cup of tea with a dash of milk; to me, it fixes anything and relaxes the body, mind, and spirit. You can wear brown when you want to be taken seriously in any type of work environment, and to invite in the respect you deserve. It can also bring wellness and simplicity to your life.

Too much brown may do the opposite. It can make you solemn, ungrounded, and undependable. Due to the color brown's changeability in nature, too much of it can lead to unpredictable behavior. Not enough brown can cause your thought patterns to wander without reason, and you may make decisions without forethought, which may not be the best for you or your family.

Brown Color Magic

While most of us do not associate the color brown with spellwork, it does have plenty of magical benefits.

For Money

Nuts draw in money, so they are great to work with when you need financial abundance. Keep a pecan nut in your wallet for your money needs. Eat cashews when money is needed, or carry them around with you. Fill a brown drawstring bag with unsalted peanuts and corn and put it in your bag, or you can leave it in the glovebox of your car.

For Protection

Put half a teaspoon of mugwort in a blue drawstring bag and carry it around with you. This will protect you from anyone that wishes you physical or spiritual harm.

To Impress at a New Job

The night before you start a new job, add a cup of pineapple juice to your bathwater. In the morning, on your way to work, chew on a cinnamon stick. This will help you make a good impression and be well-liked around the office.

For a Loving Home

To keep your home filled with love at all times, mix grains of paradise with carpet deodorizer. Sprinkle any time the home needs some tender loving care.

For Luck

If you feed the birds, luck will arrive in the strangest way. You just have to ask and you shall receive.

Planet: Mercury

Attributes: Communication, Self-Awareness, Intellect, Reliability

The color brown and the planet Mercury complement each other. Mercury is the planet to call on when you need to communicate your feelings or needs. This could be anything from being honest with a friend or family member, to declaring your love for someone, to having a positive conversation with your boss when they have been unreasonable. You can even use Mercury when asking for a pay increase!

Mercury is also the planet of reason. If you want to learn something quickly, try doing it on a Wednesday, as Mercury stimulates the mind. Mercury's practicality can come in handy when things are hard to process or when you need to find a new perspective.

Mercury is passionate about getting things done because it dislikes procrastination. Call on Mercury for even the most trivial or dreary tasks. Mercury is not only intellectual, communicative, and inventive; it can also be airy, quick-witted, and fast-paced. This is why I associate the color brown with Mercury: just like the earth, Mercury is unpredictable. We can use that to our advantage.

Day of the Week: Wednesday

On this day of the week, you can confess your wrongdoings to others without ramifications. Call it a confession from the heart and share your true feelings with others. Talk through your frustrations. This is a good day to work on your relationships at work. Are there any conversations you need to have with your employer or coworkers to improve your workplace satisfaction? Since Mercury is efficient and meticulous, if you have a task at home you hate doing, like cleaning out your closet or decluttering the garage, Wednesday is the best day to do it.

Mercury Retrograde

You've probably heard the phrase "Mercury is retrograde," but you may not know what it means. Essentially, when a planet is retrograde, it appears to move backward. It used to be believed the planet actually *was* moving backward, but we now know that isn't the case; it is just an optical illusion. This illusion muddles up a planet's energy.

So, when Mercury goes retrograde, its best attribute is affected: communication. Mercury retrograde typically lasts about three weeks. While Mercury is retrograde, you may notice more mishaps and confusion in your daily life, especially when it comes to communication. Nine times out of ten, something will go wrong during Mercury retrograde. It is like a cosmic step back. Most retrogrades feel like Mercury is testing us to see if we have learned anything.

Here are some simple things you can do to avoid the worst of Mercury retrograde.

- When working on a computer, make sure to save documents and projects frequently. You don't want to lose all your progress if your technology crashes.

- Listen before you speak. Think through what you want to say to make sure it comes out the right way.

- Doublecheck the recipient of texts and emails before hitting send.

- Do not sign any legal documents or commit to anything binding.

- Avoid making large purchases, if possible.

- I would recommend waiting to ask for a promotion or pay increase until Mercury has finished its retrograde.

- Reflect on the things that need to be changed or fixed, but don't take action yet—wait until Mercury goes direct.

- Do not cause an argument or engage in one, as they can quickly get out of hand. If you do start a fight during this time, you'll regret it.

Brown Spells with Mercury on Wednesday

This is the perfect day to do spellwork related to knowledge, honest communication, and clarity.

Spiritual Tips for Communication

Mercury has the utmost authority when it comes to communication. When you work with Mercury, you get your point across without "emotional injury," as I like to call it. You may notice that blue is used in several of these tips rather than brown. This is because blue is the color of the throat chakra, which is the communication chakra. The following tips will sharpen your communication skills on every level so that you are able to successfully get your point across in any circumstance.

- Wear something blue around your throat. This could be a scarf or a necklace with a blue crystal. Do this on a day you know your communication skills could use a boost, like when you have an important meeting or want to have a heart-to-heart. You could do this on a daily basis if you have a difficult time communicating.

- The night before a big day—a day when you will need excellent communication skills—dress light blue and brown candles with diluted myrrh essential oil, then light them. Do this as needed.

- Cleanse a carnelian agate with salt water or diluted lavender essential oil. Keep it on you at all times, or, if you're pretty confident in your ability to communicate, carry it as needed.

- Wear blue and brown clothing, especially on Wednesdays, when Mercury is ready to listen and help.

A SPELL FOR SELF-AWARENESS

A big part of being self-aware is being open-minded and taking control of your actions, thoughts, and feelings. We can become more aware just by listening to our intuition or exercising. Other ways to increase self-awareness are daily meditation, paying attention to others, and being nonjudgmental. This spell can also improve our self-awareness.

1. In your sacred space, dress four brown candles and one white candle with diluted frankincense essential oil. As you do this, ask yourself if you are self-aware. Reflect on how you could improve.

2. Make a circle out of the brown candles. In the middle of the circle, place the white candle. Light them all while saying:

I am aware of my actions, thoughts, and feelings

3. Place a clear quartz crystal and a carnelian agate in front of the candles. Sprinkle nutmeg powder on top of the crystals and say:

I will be nonjudgmental about all things, even myself

4. Visualize the candles' flames penetrating the crystals and charging them with the energy of self-awareness.

5. Once the candles have burned themselves out, pick up the crystals and place them in a light brown drawstring bag. Carry the crystals with you for as long as you feel you need them; use them again as needed.

A Spell to Boost Your Intellect

Most of us wish we were smarter in one area or another. For some of us, we wish we understood math better; others may struggle with writing. There is always room to improve. Acquiring knowledge doesn't happen overnight, but this spell can sharpen your mind.

1. Find an old dictionary around the house. If you don't have one, ask a family member or friend. They can also be purchased online or from used bookstores.

2. Dress two brown candles with diluted lemon essential oil, then light them.

3. Sit in front of the candles and open the dictionary to the letter A, then flip to the letter B, and so on until you get to Z. Say:

Now I know everything from A to Z

4. Close the dictionary and leave it near the candles until they have consumed. Then place the dictionary on your bedside table as a reminder of your intelligence.

A Spell to Increase Someone's Reliability

There is nothing worse than being consistently let down by someone who is not reliable. This could be a child that never remembers to do their chores, a friend who cancels plans last minute, or a partner that conveniently finds something else that needs to be done as soon as there are dirty dishes to wash. I think you are getting the gist of the reliability I'm going on about.

Typically, I do not recommend doing spells for someone else without getting their permission first. However, for things like this, I like to use modification spells, which are not negative or harmful to whomever they are directed toward. This spell's simplicity is what makes it so ideal. If you do this spell on Mercury's day, Wednesday, you can't go wrong.

1. On a brown piece of paper, write the following:

**I, <u>(name)</u>, modify you, <u>(name)</u>,
to keep your promise to <u>(task)</u>.**

Keep in mind that this will only work if the person already knows what you want them to modify. What I mean by this is, it's important to make sure the situation is already on that person's radar. For example, if you want your partner to start picking up the mail after work but have not discussed this with him, he probably won't start getting the mail all of a sudden. Modifications can be tricky if you haven't had an outright conversation about the issue. I suppose what I'm trying to say is that people should be aware of the change they need to make—this is when magic is most effective.

2. Once you've finished writing, add peppermint leaves and a few drops of peppermint essential oil on top of the paper.

3. Roll up the paper with the peppermint leaves inside. Wrap a white ribbon around it to make sure the leaves don't fall out. Keep this with you as a reminder that modification is taking place.

4. Once you feel that this person is reliable again, unroll the paper and let the leaves fall on the grass. The paper can go in the bin. Redo the spell as needed.

11
Black

In the past, you may have mixed many paint colors together to get the color black. Interestingly enough, black is the absence of light, so technically speaking, it is also the absence of color.

For many, black is a sad color; it's often associated with funerals and emotional sorrow. Understandably, some see this as a lonely color. Others see black as a rebellious color; it can be representative of a defiant nature.

Whatever your personal feelings about the color black, it is a fantastic color to use in your magic. Black is beautiful, sincere, and strong. It demands the power it engenders.

Black can be a sedative that makes you dismiss the important things around you. You may lack confidence or feelings of positivity. The color black can make you aggressive, heighten feelings of depression, or make you feel really negative about yourself or those around you, sometimes to the point of paranoia.

Everyday Uses of Black

In magic, black wards off negativity and can be worn for protection. It defends us from negative workings and brings truth to magical workings. This color can even be used to remove hexes, banish unwanted influences, and break spells. Black items are must-haves in all households because they provide a shield from negativity.

If we surround ourselves with too much black, it can cause aggressiveness and rebellion, not to mention fear. If there is not enough black in your home, you may feel unprotected, not to mention doubtful and insecure.

BLACK COLOR MAGIC

This is the most protective color that you can use in spellwork.

TO BANISH EVIL FROM YOUR HOME

When you feel that there are evil spirits around, light a black candle and wish them gone. Then light an orange candle and wish them a home that is not yours—preferably one in the heavens above.

TO REDUCE NEGATIVITY

If you feel that your home is weighed down by negativity, light black and white candles every Saturday, just before dawn, to get rid of it. You can even get rid of your own negativity by lighting a black and a white candle at the same time.

TO RELEASE HATRED

To truly hate someone requires you to block out every single ounce of good energy in your life. To release all the hatred you are carrying, including the hatred you may not *know* you are carrying, light a black candle and a white candle while wishing for peace in your heart. This will help bring good energy back into your life.

FOR PROTECTION SPRAY

Ask permission to take three leaves from an oak tree. Then, put the three leaves, seven rusty nails, a small handful of fresh rue, water, and two drops of blue food coloring into a spray bottle. Let it sit outside in the sun for a day. When you want to use the spray, spritz it in front of you, then walk through it. This is the best protection spray I do—it's like walking into a protection cloud that is with you all day.

Planet: Saturn

Attributes: Justice, Banishing, Protection

If you are not a responsible person, one way or the other, Saturn will make sure you become one. The planet Saturn is disciplinary, determined, and just. It likes things in their proper place—Saturn can't handle disorder or injustice.

Saturn is considered the karmic planet. There is no middle of the road with Saturn: there is only right or wrong. I think of Saturn as a law enforcer and the defender of the innocent. I recommend working with Saturn when combating negativity, whether it is due to magic or another person. For example, if you're dealing with a bully, ask Saturn to influence your magic. Think of Saturn as your knight in shining armor.

Day of the Week: Saturday

Saturday is a great day to release whatever is weighing on you. This is a great day of the week to organize: get rid of the old to make room for the new. This applies to energy work too—make this day your banishing day. Cleanse your house with incense to get rid of stagnant energy. Add banishing essences or herbs to a mop bucket to wash negativity out of the house while leaving clean, positive energy in your wake. Protect what is yours from intentional (and unintentional) negativity by doing some simple spells. This is a terrific day to combat dark forces and spirits.

This day of the week keeps us grounded. Spend a Saturday finishing a long-overdue project, studying for a test, or asking those older than you for advice. Try to listen with an open mind all day; consider scenarios you never thought possible.

BLACK SPELLS WITH SATURN ON SATURDAY

I love doing protective magic on Saturdays because I know Saturn doubles the strength of my magic, and I use this to my advantage.

SPIRITUAL TIPS TO REPEL NEGATIVE ENERGY

People are the ultimate spiritual vacuum cleaner. We can pick up negative energy from just about anyone or anything. Most of the time, we don't even know it! Negative energy is like a foreign body; think of it as a leech that latches on to your spiritual vessel. When things are constantly going wrong, you know something negative has attached itself to you.

There are many ways to get rid of negative energy that do not involve a spell. If you had to do a spell every time you felt you'd been invaded by a negative force, you'd need a new budget for candles!

Here are a few ways you can quickly dislodge unwanted energy or protect against it.

- Take salt baths on Saturdays.

- Embellish a garlic wreath with a black ribbon. Hang it inside or outside your front door.

- Always have a black crystal with you. They all repel negative energy. For an extra boost, program a black crystal for that specific reason.

- Place a bowl of uncooked rice where the family gathers.

- Burn frankincense incense on your censer as often as you can.

- Take note of those who are always commenting that they wish they had what you have.

- Cleanse a tiger's eye crystal and take it to your workplace. Keep it at your desk or another personal place. This will protect you from negativity around the office.

- Black is protective, so wear black whenever you know you are going into a negative situation.

A SPELL TO HALT SOMEONE WHO WISHES YOU HARM

I wish everyone had others' best interests at heart. Unfortunately, that simply isn't the case, and most of the time, we haven't done anything to deserve the harsh treatment we receive. In my experience, 98 percent of the time, someone wishing you ill is jealous or driven by their ego. Fortunately, this spell can stop those sorts of situations from escalating.

1. Dress two white candles and one black candle with coconut oil.

2. Light your charcoal tablet. Place a few leaves of sage and dragons blood resin on top. Let the smoke engulf your sacred space.

3. Light the black candle. Watch the flame and envision it melting everything the person has done or is capable of doing. Say:

I know you wish me harm, but this is where it stops

4. Light the white candles. Say:

Go in peace and leave me alone
And never harm me or any other
With your evil, harmful thoughts

5. Get a cup of uncooked rice and pour it around the candles. As you do, say:

Every grain of rice is a week of
protection for me and those I love
From you

6. Let the candles be consumed. Then, scoop up the rice and sprinkle it outside your front and back doors.

A Spell for Addiction

In one way or another, we all suffer from an addiction, but some are more harmful than others.[2] You might be addicted to television, coffee, or exercise, or your addiction may be more destructive. Addictions to drugs, alcohol, and cigarettes are spiritually and physically damaging.

This spell can be done for yourself, or you can perform this spell for a loved one with the intent of helping them come to terms with their addiction so that they can begin the healing process. If you are doing this for a loved one or friend, seek their permission before doing this spell.

1. In your sacred space, dress two black candles and one red candle with diluted bay leaf essential oil. Clear your mind so that your only thoughts are of the addiction that needs to come to an end. Visualize what life was like before the addiction.

2. Light the red candle, visualizing the courage and strength needed to navigate the withdrawal process.

2. If you, a family member, or a friend is suffering with some type of addiction, please consult loved ones, a medical practitioner, or a group such as Alcoholics Anonymous. There are support groups for all kinds of addictions. Once you have decided you want to stop, you have already taken one big step toward recovery. There is nothing to be ashamed of; please ask for help.

3. Light the two black candles, visualizing the addiction melting away with the flames.

4. Write the addiction down on a piece of paper, then cross it out until the words cannot be seen.

5. In a black cloth, wrap up the piece of paper or a representation of the addiction (e.g., if it's nicotine, wrap a cigarette in the black cloth). Tie the cloth closed with black ribbon.

6. If this spell is for you, hold the bundle in your hands and say:

Never to be seen
And not to be used and abused again

If this spell is for a loved one, hold the bundle in your hands and say:

I know you can do this
I wish you would stop the abuse
And seek support to fight your addiction

7. Spend some time visualizing the hurt others are going through because of the addiction. Imagine the candles' flames melting away sadness and suffering.

8. Let all the candles consume to the end. Bury the black bundle in a potted plant that is wilting, one that you know will recover

with enough love and tender care. As you bury the bundle, visualize the addiction once more.

A Spell to Silence Gossip

People can't help but to gossip. There is benign gossip, and then there is malignant gossip, the kind of gossip that, unfortunately, transfers via negative energy and causes emotional and physical havoc. If you are the victim of gossip and you know the person spreading harmful lies about you, let's make them stop.

1. On a piece of parchment paper, write the name of the person spreading the gossip. Do this with a black pen.

2. Place the piece of paper on top of a black cloth, then sprinkle sandalwood powder on the person's name. Add seven cooking cloves.

3. Wrap up the bundle as if it were an envelope. To hold it together, use safety pins. As you form the bundle, say:

Your tongue is darkened by your spiteful nature
Find something better to do than
spread malicious gossip about me

4. Keep this bundle in a special place where no one can touch it for at least seven days.

5. After at least a week has passed, take the black bundle to a body of water. Let the bundle be carried away by the water. The gossip's lips will be zipped.

A Spell to Banish Self-Doubt

We all doubt ourselves from time to time, but you must have faith in your abilities. Whenever you feel like you are losing faith in yourself, try this spell.

1. Get a sewing pin and a black candle. Using the pin, write your self-doubt on the candle.

2. Grab a white candle. Using the same pin, write what you want to replace your self-doubt with (examples: confidence, strength, fearlessness).

3. Once finished, dress the candles with a drop of olive oil, visualizing the doubt you are banishing and what its replacement is going to be.

4. Light the black candle first, then make a circle around it with peppermint leaves.

5. Light the white candle, then make a circle around it with sage leaves.

6. Look at the two flames side by side. Visualize the black candle banishing your self-doubt and the white one absorbing that energy and replacing it. Say:

> **As these candles burn, they will banish self-doubt and replace it with (word)**

Part II
Color Magic in Everyday Life

Many of us take Mother Nature's beauty for granted. Be honest with yourself: when was the last time you were outdoors and really looked at your surroundings? We need to pay more attention to the earth's natural beauty. Nature has graciously given us so many different shapes, textures, and colors! This section of the book focuses on Mother Nature's gifts to us, specifically crystal spells and ways to incorporate the water element. I will also share ways to utilize the magic in everyday items we may overlook, such as the color of a towel.

We'll talk a lot about crystals in this section of the book. Rocks are one of Mother Nature's most beautiful gifts, and they are all around us. For example, Ayers Rock, best known to Australians as Uluru, is one of Australia's most-visited tourist attractions. It's an inselberg, which is essentially a hill that rises out of nowhere. Uluru is a huge formation—I drove around it once. It has a perimeter of almost six miles and is over one thousand feet high. This giant rock is a coarse-grained sandstone rich in feldspar and quartz. For those that don't know, feldspar is a mineral, and minerals form crystals.

One interesting thing about Uluru is that it changes color during sunrise and sunset. In the mornings, it looks purple and gray at times. At midday, it looks red. At night, the red fades and turns to pink, then purple, until the sun sets on the horizon. Uluru is one of the many wonders of Mother Nature. I've shared this with you because the next chapter is all about doing spells with crystals. Minerals—crystals—may look ordinary at first, but once they are cut and polished, their luster surfaces. And when faceted, crystals are a site to behold.

Just like crystals, water is a big part of this section of the book. The water element brings resilience to any type of magical working. When I think of water, I think of Victoria Falls in Africa. The water cascades down, causing a mist of spray. The droplets refract light and create magnificent rainbows. Water spells, specifically bath spells, are like your own tiny version of Victoria Falls. Baths are a great way to bring in positive energy, and they can even wash away negative energy. The bath spells in this section add colors, herbs, flowers, and even tea bags to water, and the resulting mixtures are magical.

This part of the book ends with a chapter on finding the magic in everyday items we take for granted. I will share easy, approachable ways to add color magic to everyday life. For example, with a magical mindset, stopping at a traffic light is an opportunity to quickly visualize your needs. But we'll talk more about that later!

Every color has a mission and a designation. Without color, life would be boring! It brings so much brightness to our lives.

12
Crystals

All over the earth, colorful minerals and rocks can be found deep within the soil. They have literally rocked our world since the beginning of time, and when polished or made into jewelry, their beauty truly shines.

Today, the legacy of crystals is stronger than ever before. Crystals play a big part in magical workings. Their colors and properties are endless. You can use crystals to enhance spiritual enlightenment, boost psychic abilities, aid conventional medicine, attract wealth, tap in to your power, protect yourself, deepen self-love, and so much more.

Like a candle in the midst of darkness, crystals provide us with a sense of comfort and acceptance that warms the heart. They exude love and compassion. Ultimately, crystals help us better understand ourselves and the world around us. When used in magic, a crystal's energy amplifies to help manifest your needs.

Crystal Spells

When I add crystals to my magical practice, I am ten times more engaged. Crystal spells are a fun way to stay focused on your intent. When you work with crystals, you are actually working with vibrant energies that are just waiting to be activated with your needs.

For Psychic Workings: Amber

Cleanse an amber crystal with frankincense essential oil. Use it for any type of psychic workings, when learning how to read the tarot, or when communicating with spirits. You can also hold an amber crystal while meditating for deeper understanding of things that concern you.

For Protection: Carnelian

On the night of the full moon, let a carnelian crystal sit in the grass all night and into the morning. Then hold the crystal in your hand and visualize the protection you are seeking. Say:

Brown and orange crystal
Protect me from those who wish mischief
or accidents that can cause me harm
And lead them away from my physical and spiritual self

In a little blue pouch, place about a teaspoon of fresh sage and a few pieces of palo santo, then add the crystal. As long as you have this pouch with you, it will protect you.

To Get Rid of Negative Energy: Bloodstone

On a Saturday, write down all of the negative energy you wish to rid yourself of. Place this piece of paper inside a small bowl. Add two teaspoons of brown sugar while visualizing your needs. Gently place a bloodstone crystal inside the bowl and cover the whole thing with a blue cloth.

In your sacred space, light a blue candle and set it next to the bowl. Let it consume, then take the crystal out and place it by your bedside. The negative energy you wrote about will be removed.

For Dependency: Amethyst

On a Tuesday, cleanse an amethyst crystal with two drops of vinegar. Hold it in your hands and visualize the dependency you want to release. (This could be anything you have an unhealthy attachment to, such as alcohol.)

In your sacred space, dress a pink candle with olive oil. Light it while visualizing the love within you, which will help you through this trying time.

Place the amethyst crystal inside a clear glass, then add a handful of fresh rue and a dash of salt. Fill the glass with distilled water. While mixing this together, say:

Everything that I'm dependent on
Will never enter my front door

Place a black cloth on top of the glass and snuff the candle out when finished.

Take the glass into your backyard and leave it on the grass for the night. (If you don't have a backyard, you can leave it on your balcony.) The next day, pour the contents of the glass in the bin, but make sure to take the crystal out first. Carry the crystal with you until the dependency is gone.

For Stress: Amethyst

Keep an amethyst crystal inside a blue pouch with a handful of lavender buds. Hang it around your neck to keep you cool, calm, and collected in even the most stressful situations.

To Strengthen Your Aura: Clear Quartz

In your sacred space, anoint a clear quartz crystal with lavender essential oil. Dress a white candle with olive oil, then light it.

As the candle burns, sit as if you were meditating. Hold the crystal in your right hand (or your left hand, if you are left-handed) and visualize your aura. Imagine it is a color that corresponds with your needs. Send your wish to the Universe.

Do this for about fifteen to twenty minutes whenever the need arises. This is an excellent way to enforce your aura with universal light and strength.

To Cool Hot Tempers: Blue Lace Agate

On a piece of paper, write the name of the person with the bad temper. Place the paper inside a light blue drawstring bag, then add a large pinch of fresh, aromatic sage leaves.

Hold a blue lace agate crystal and rub a few drops of bergamot essential oil on it. While you do this, think only of the person you are doing the spell for. See them at peace, finding calmness and not getting upset, even in the worst-case scenario.

Set the drawstring bag outside under a waning moon. Ask the moon to decrease the person's anger.

Place the drawstring bag under the person's bed and wait for a much-needed peaceful change. If this person does not live with you, place the bag in your sacred space, away from your magical tools, in the name of the person who needs to control their anger.

For a Broken Heart: Rose Quartz

Place a rose quartz crystal in a glass of salt water for one day and one night.

From a pink silk cloth, cut out two heart shapes, then start to stitch the shapes together. While you do this, visualize your broken heart mending with every stitch. Leave a small opening and place the following inside: the rose quartz, petals from a pink rose, and seven cooking cloves. Once finished, stitch the opening closed.

Place your new heart under your pillow. Leave it there as your real heart mends. You could also carry the pouch with you as close to your own heart as possible.

For Strength: Onyx

Light a red candle while visualizing the strength you need, then add a few drops of ginger essential oil to an onyx crystal. Wrap a red ribbon around the crystal until you

have a nice little bundle—the crystal shouldn't be visible. As you are doing this, visualize the strength you wish you had. Carry this with you for strength in moments of weakness.

For Compassion: Garnet

Cleanse a garnet crystal with baby oil. Hold the crystal in your hands and wish for the compassion you need or the compassion you want another person to have. Carry the garnet with you always or, if it is not you that needs more compassion, give it to the person that does.

For Creativity: Smoky Quartz

On a yellow piece of paper, write about the creativity you wish you had. Then wrap a smoky quartz crystal in the paper. Keep the bundle in a yellow or orange pouch and your newfound creativity will shine.

To Prevent Danger: Malachite

Hold a malachite crystal in your hand and add two drops of frankincense essential oil. Visualize the danger you feel is upon you, then dismiss it from happening. Carry the malachite in a black pouch to prevent danger from manifesting.

For Fidelity: Tiger's Eye

Place a tiger's eye crystal in a glass and add water and a tablespoon of salt. Leave this outside for three days and three nights. Make sure the moon is full on one of those nights. After enough time has passed, rub your hands together, then hold the crystal in your hands. Think about who has been unfaithful and ask for them to remain devoted. Keep the tiger's eye close to you so its energies will transfer to the one who strays.

For Memorable Dreams: Labradorite

Smear a labradorite crystal with diluted jasmine essential oil. Hold the crystal in your hand and visualize yourself remembering your dreams. Then place the crystal, a teaspoon of jasmine flowers, and a teaspoon of mugwort inside a white sock. Place the sock under your pillow, and the dreams you'll have will be clear as day.

For Endurance: Jade

Cleanse a jade crystal in the sun for at least three hours. Then hold it in your hands and visualize the physical or spiritual endurance you desire. This crystal is strongest when worn, especially around the neck.

For Energy: Citrine, Clear Quartz, and Hematite

Place citrine, clear quartz, and hematite crystals outside, in the sunlight. Once the three crystals are hot to the touch, place them inside a red drawstring bag. Hold the bag in your hands and visualize the energy you need. Carry the pouch with you when you feel your energy levels running low.

For Better Sleep: Amethyst and Azurite

Cleanse an amethyst crystal and an azurite crystal with frankincense essential oil, then place them inside a blue cotton sock. Inside the sock, add a large pinch of valerian and a few drops of lavender essential oil.

Mix it all together. As you do, visualize not waking up during the night. Place the sock under your pillow. It may take a day or so for this spell to work, so please be patient.

For True Love: Rose Quartz

Cleanse a rose quartz crystal on the night of the full moon. Set it in a glass of water and add a teaspoon of salt and a few drops of rose essential oil. Place the glass outside. In the morning, bring it in and hold it in your hands, visualizing the love you want to feel for yourself or another.

Pour the contents of the glass out, then place the rose quartz inside a pink pouch with a few pink rose petals, cardamon seeds, and two fluffy pink craft balls. Carry the pouch with you during the day. At night, place it under your pillow. If you are consistent, true love will find you.

For Money: Pyrite and Red Jasper
Cleanse a pyrite crystal and a red jasper crystal with hot water and salt. Once dry, place them inside a green pouch made of cotton, then fill the pouch with sesame seeds. Hold the pouch in your hands and visualize money and abundance coming into your life. Let the Universe show you places you never thought money could be found.

Watercolor Crystal Infusions

Did you know that when you add crystals to colored glasses (or existing water bottles) with a few drops of food coloring, which is nontoxic, it will cause a magical effect? Sometimes I have three or four different color bottles in my fridge depending on what I need at that particular time.

When you drink water that has been infused with the magic of crystals and color, you are using color visually *and* internally. Every time you take a mouthful of water that you have infused, that splash of color spreads through your body and to your aura, manifesting positive changes or expelling what you don't want or need in your life.

First things first: there are a lot of crystals out there, and unfortunately, some are toxic. In this section, I am only recommending crystals I know are safe and that I have used in many water infusions in the past. Always use tumbled crystals in infusions. Tumbled stones have polished, rounded surfaces. If the stone is chipped, find a different one—one that is smooth—before adding it to an infusion.

Make sure you cleanse a crystal before adding it to an infusion. Clean the crystal with soap and water, then let it air-dry on a paper towel. Once it is dry, hold the crystal in your hand and visualize what you need. This will activate the crystal. Once your crystal is ready to go, fill a glass bottle with water and add food coloring, if needed. You can fill the bottle with tap or filtered water; it is up to you.

A crystal does not change the composition of water, but it does make water taste different; I would say it tastes a bit more alkaline. This tells us that the water has been changed, though this change is invisible to the naked eye. Infused water is magically charged and ready to help you achieve your goals.

Some crystals dissolve or deteriorate in water, and this is not safe to drink. Before adding a crystal to an infusion, please research that particular crystal to make sure it is nontoxic and water-safe (insoluble). All the infusions shared in this section use nontoxic, insoluble crystals.

Once you have made your infusion and are ready to drink it, be mindful of the crystals in the water. *Do not swallow the crystals when drinking any of the infusions.* I recommend drinking your infusion through a straw to be extra careful. If you live with other people—especially if you have children in the home—make sure you are the only one drinking out of this bottle. Label the bottle, caution others that there are crystals inside, or keep it somewhere safe.

I usually make large batches of infused water and store the leftovers. That way, I have infusions ready whenever I need them. You can put your crystal infusions in the fridge, store them somewhere safe, or carry them with you as you go about your day. Whenever you drink infused water, remember to take a moment to visualize what you want the water to help you with.

For Positivity or Protection:
Obsidian and a Black Bottle

When you feel negativity consuming you, or when you notice your emotions are more negative than usual, use this infusion to see the positive side of things. You can also use it as a protection tool if you think that someone may be using magic to weaken your physical health.

I recommend using a black glass bottle for this infusion. With that being said, it is hard to find a black glass bottle, so if you can't, that is okay.

Fill a black bottle with water and add two drops of black food coloring and an obsidian crystal.

For Better Communication, More Peace, or Less Anger: Blue Lace Agate and a Blue Bottle

Use this infusion when you are having problems communicating with others for whatever reason—it will help you open up. You could also drink this infusion an hour before bed to fall asleep easier. I like to use this infusion when I feel angry; it calms my mind and my senses. The infusion can help you verbalize why you are angry so that you can find peace within.

Fill a blue bottle with water, then add a blue lace agate. Depending on the size of the bottle, add one or two drops of blue food coloring.

For Health or Meditation:
Clear Quartz and a Clear Bottle

Drink this water when you are dealing with health issues. It can help with something short-term, like a hospital stay, or something more long-term, such as a chronic condition. You can drink this infusion before meditating to alert your body to the journey you are about to take.

Fill a clear bottle with water, then add two clear quartz crystals. Close the bottle and leave it outside in the grass for a day. If you do not have a yard, set it inside a potted plant, as the bottle just needs to be on top of some soil to absorb the earth element.

For Healing the Heart or Abundance:
Aventurine and a Green Bottle

I love this infusion! It helps repair a broken heart, heals painful emotions, and allows us to release the past that still haunts us. While you drink this infusion, visualize what difficult emotions or memories you want to leave behind. This is also a great infusion to drink if you want more abundance in your life.

Fill a green bottle with water. Add an aventurine crystal and a drop of green food coloring.

For Finding Love or the Love Within:
Rose Quartz and a Pink Bottle

If you struggle with low self-esteem, try this infusion. Every time you take a drink, it'll kickstart the love within. Start drinking this water every morning; soon, you will be more compassionate, kind, and loving to yourself. You can also use this infusion if you are searching for true love.

Fill a pink bottle with water. Infuse it with two rose quartz crystals and two drops of pink food coloring. As you drink from the bottle, visualize the love you want to feel.

For Spiritual and Psychic Work:
Amethyst and a Purple Bottle

This infusion aids with spirit-world communication. Most of us wish we could hear our guides and angels more clearly, especially when we are in need of their advice. Before doing a meditation to ask your guides or angels questions, drink this water to make communication easier.

Fill a purple bottle with water, then add two amethyst crystals and two drops of purple food coloring. Leave the bottle outside for one night, preferably under the full moon.

For Courage: Garnet and a Red Bottle

This infusion taps into your inner strength so it is easier for you to express your courageous spirit.

Fill a red bottle with water. Add a garnet crystal and a drop of red food coloring. If the water looks more pink than red, add another drop. Drink this infusion on a Tuesday. Keep drinking it every day until the courage needed surfaces within you.

For Learning and Remembering: Citrine and a Yellow Bottle

I like to recommend this infusion to anyone who needs to remember something, whether that is procedures at a new job or formulas for a math class. I recommend drinking this wise and intelligent water during an exam—people will only see a yellow bottle. And when the crystals clink together, it'll sound like ice cubes.

Fill a yellow bottle with water. Add two drops of yellow food coloring and three citrine crystals.

13
Magical Color Sprays

You may think of water as "just water," but the water we drink, the water we shower or cook with, even the water we flush down the toilet, is much more than that! Water is an element, and like all elements, it has its own special magical properties. When you add color to water, it transforms into a magical medium, allowing conversation between you and the Universe, and its uses are endless.

I like to use color in spray bottles to cause an effect. For the sprays in this chapter, you will need to purchase a few glass spray bottles and various colors of food coloring. You would be surprised how many food coloring options are out there now that baking has become such a colorful industry! Food coloring comes in small plastic bottles, either individually or in a pack.

For Protection: Black

In a spray bottle, add bottled water and rosemary leaves, then add a few drops of black food coloring. Let it stand for a few hours, then spray it around the outside of your home to protect against unwanted negative energies.

For Healing: Blue

In a spray bottle, add tap water, two drops of blue food coloring, and fresh fennel. Leave it outside for the night. In the morning, spray the mixture around the house and on your skin for healing to occur. While you do this, visualize being healthy, and imagine the spray protecting you from illness. Do this as often as needed.

For Peace: Purple

In a spray bottle, add three drops of lavender essential oil and lavender leaves. Fill the bottle with bottled water, then add two drops of lavender food coloring. Spray this essence when there is upheaval to calm all the destructive energies in your home.

For Financial Abundance: Green

Add green food coloring and fresh basil to a spray bottle filled with bottled water. Shake gently. Spray this around the house when finances are dwindling and could use a boost.

For Spirit Communication: Orange

For open communication with a deity, fill a spray bottle with bottled water. Add two drops of orange essential oil, an orange slice, and two drops of orange food coloring. Place this bottle in your sacred space and light a white candle. Close your eyes and think of the spirit communication you are seeking, then spray this essence around you. Visualize this vibrant color opening the door to the spirit world so you can deliver your message.

For Encouragement: Orange

In a spray bottle, add bottled water, a small handful of rosemary leaves, and two drops of rosemary essential oil. If you need encouragement, spray this under your bed for seven nights. If someone you live with needs encouragement, spray it under their bed for seven nights without them knowing; you'll notice the difference a few days later.

For Love: Pink

Find a small spray bottle you can carry in your purse. Inside this bottle, add one tablespoon of vodka, the seeds from a red apple that you have eaten, five basil leaves, one tiny piece of a cinnamon stick, a drop of spearmint essential oil, one drop of pink food coloring, and five drops of lavender essential oil. Fill the spray bottle with bottled water. Spray yourself three times a day, always thinking about the love you want to attract. Once the bottle is out of water, toss the old ingredients in the bin and prepare the spray again, using fresh ingredients. You can use the same bottle as before.

For Passion: Red

Fill a spray bottle with bottled water. Add fresh thyme and two drops of red food coloring. Keep the bottle on your desk at work or at home. When you are feeling lukewarm about your job, spray this mixture around your workspace to find the passion you used to have. This spray will also help you find strength to overcome obstacles and will reinforce your professionalism so that you can handle any issues that may arise.

For Intuition: Yellow

Fill a spray bottle with bottled water. Add two drops of yellow food coloring, two drops of peppermint essential oil, and two drops of frankincense essential oil. After every shower, towel dry and then spray your upper stomach. Gently rub the spray in a clockwise direction to inspire your solar plexus chakra. This will keep you from making the same mistakes you made in the past.

14
Color Baths

Water makes life on Earth possible, and it also keeps us alive; humans can only go a few days without water. Water nourishes the earth and the body, so just think how much it can nourish our emotional well-being as well! When we use water within the laws of magic, its benefits are endless. But before calling on the water element, make sure you respect it. Water is incredibly powerful: it gives life, but it can also take it away. Be mindful of the support water freely gives us; don't take it for granted.

Work with the water element to cleanse the soul and soothe turbulent emotions. Any time you soak in water (bathtub, ocean, river, etc.), you can use the water's flow to carry away old emotions or to invite in new energy.

When you want to release your worries, let them disappear down the drain. When you need to accept something heavy, allow water to help you carry it.

Taking a bath after a stressful day can calm the mind and relax tight muscles. But with a little bit of spellwork, baths can have even more potent effects. Once you add a pinch of herbs and a few drops of food coloring to bathwater, your tub becomes a magical space. The water in the bath is no longer just bathwater: it's a magical fountain, ready to help you with your needs.

Here are some things to remember about color baths.

- Find out if your bathtub is porous or nonporous. If your tub is porous, food coloring will stain it. In that case, if a spell calls for food coloring, add a piece of colored cloth to the water instead.

- Place a nonslip mat in the bath so you do not hurt yourself when getting in or out of the water.

- Always wet your hair during the bath.

- When you remove the bath plug, visualize the water taking any negative energy to the depths of the sewer, where it belongs.

- After the tub has drained, collect any remaining magical ingredients. Dispose of used ingredients, like herbs or tea bags, and cleanse any reusable ingredients, like crystals.

- Pat yourself dry to seal the bath's energy within you. Pat dry with white towels if you can, but be prepared for them to get stained if your bath included food coloring. If you don't want to stain any towels, you can pat dry with something else; even paper towels will do.

Think of these baths as a water salad: you will be tossing in all kinds of ingredients, and they complement each other so well! Enjoy these magical water salads.

For Negative Energy

1. On a Saturday, dress a white candle and a black candle with olive oil. Take them to the bathroom and light them as your bath fills with warm water. Visualize the black candle absorbing the negative

energy you want gone and the white candle giving you strength.

2. Add fresh basil leaves (lots of them), a few sticks of cinnamon, three drops of pink food coloring, four drops of lime essential oil, and a cup of bath salts to your bathwater.

3. Get into the bath and relax. Spend a moment visualizing the negative energy you are carrying. Rub the basil and cinnamon all over your body. Let the salt wipe away all negative energy, be it yours or someone else's.

4. When you get out of the bath, snuff the candles so they can be used again. Do not rinse your hair or body—just pat yourself dry to seal the energy within you.

5. Repeat this process for three days.

For Money

I love money baths. They are so much fun! You can do this spell whenever money is needed, preferably on a Sunday or Thursday.

1. Take as many tealights to the bathroom as you'd like. Light them while thinking of your money needs. Remember, don't

be too narrowly focused; a phrase like "I want to win the lottery" does not leave you open to other opportunities. As the wax melts, add a drop of green food coloring to each candle.

2. In a waterproof jug, add the following tea bags: English breakfast, chamomile, jasmine, and ginger. Fill the jug with boiling water, then add three drops of green food coloring. Let this steep for about five minutes, then strain this mixture and add it to your bath, setting aside the tea bags.

3. Add a teaspoon of allspice, a few nuts (it doesn't matter which kind, as they are all good for money), and one or two drops of clove essential oil to your bathwater.

4. With the lights down and the green tealight candles burning, enter this money tea bag bath. Enjoy the scents and their properties, spending time visualizing your money needs.

5. When you get out of the bath, seal the energy within you by patting dry. After draining the tub, pick up all the nuts and tea bags and let them dry.

6. Once dry, open the tea bags and empty them on a patch of grass. Scatter the nuts around the area as well.

For Love

1. Light a few pink candles (you can pick the number) and dress them with lavender essential oil. As you do, visualize the love you want to manifest. Ask yourself if this spell is to find inner love or whether it is to attract love.

2. Once you've determined what kind of spell you'd like to do, light the candles while thinking of love. Start to fill your tub with warm water.

3. Add all kinds of fresh, pink flower petals to this bath. You could even mix in white rose petals or gardenia petals. Also add three drops of pink food coloring, a few drops of geranium essential oil, and a few strawberries (as many as twelve).

4. Get into the bath and submerge your whole body in the water. Bring the petals and the strawberries closer to you and gently run them through your fingers. Feel the energy of the bathwater connecting to your body.

5. Once you're finished in the bath, pat dry and gather all the strawberries and petals. Take them to a beautiful garden so the earth can return them to its bosom.

For Health

This bath is best done on Mondays.

1. In your bathroom, dress a white candle and a blue candle with fennel oil. As you dress the candles, visualize yourself as healthy.

2. Prepare your bath and add several drops of yellow food coloring. Add a bunch of fresh thyme to the water as well as all the yellow flower petals you can get your hands on.

3. Submerge yourself in this healing water and visualize all that is needed to make you healthy again. This could be general, like time, or it could be specific, like a medical treatment. Take as much time as needed, keeping your thoughts centered on a healthy outcome.

4. When you're ready to drain the tub, watch the water disappear along with your health issues. Pat dry. Pick up the flower petals and thyme and put them in the bin.

For Protection

I recommend doing this spell on a Saturday.

1. Dress a black candle, a blue candle, and a white candle with patchouli essential oil while visualizing the protection you are seeking, then light them.

2. Draw a hot bath and add several drops of blue food coloring.

3. In a large, blue organza bag, place seven rusty nails (the bigger the better) and a handful of black peppercorns. After cinching the bag closed, add it to the bathwater. Let the bag infuse the water with its protective concoction for a few minutes.

4. Before getting into the bath, add three drops of basil essential oil. Once the water temperature is to your liking, get in while visualizing the protection you need.

5. Pick up the organza bag and gently rub your body with it, visualizing this mix wrapping you in a layer of invisible protection that is impregnable by negative energies.

6. Stay in the water as long as you'd like. When you unplug the drain, stand up and gently rub the bag all over your body once again, then pat yourself dry.

7. Let this organza bag dry under the sun, then keep it under your pillow. As long as it is there, you will be protected. You can also rub yourself with the bag when you feel extra protection is needed.

For Relaxation

This bath can help ease your worries, stress, and negative emotions. It can be repeated as often as you need!

1. Get around ten star anise and bring them to a boil—the scent alone should be enough to start to calm you.

2. Start filling your bath with water. Add the now-boiled star anise and its infused water, a few drops of blue food coloring, and a few drops of bergamot essential oil. Then add fresh mint, basil, and parsley.

3. Set as many candles around the bathroom as you'd like. You can use any color(s). There's no need to dress the candles, but when you light them, visualize being relaxed and think about what stressors you wish to get rid of.

4. Play some soft and relaxing music, then get in the bath.

5. Close your eyes and visualize the stresses of the day being scrubbed away by the contents in the water. Gently rub the spell ingredients on your shoulders, neck, and lower back. Stay in the water as long as you'd like.

6. When you drain the tub, visualize all your stresses going down the drain. Pat dry. Take the leftover ingredients out of the tub and put them in the bin.

For Anger

Anger prevents spiritual growth, and it can affect our relationships, employment, and even friendships. This bath is all about letting go of frustrations that cause anger deep within us, and it can be repeated whenever you feel anger beginning to dominate your emotions.

1. Dress a red candle and a blue candle with olive oil. While you do this, visualize what is making you angry. Think about why you need to let it go. Light the red candle first. See your anger being consumed by the candle. Light the blue candle and let the peace and tranquil-

ity it offers keep you safe. See your anger being wrapped in a blue bubble of peace and quiet. Start running your bath while reflecting on your anger.

2. Add a few drops of purple food coloring, a few drops of eucalyptus and fennel essential oils, and a full cup of bath salts to the water.

3. Once you get in the bath, visualize the salt stripping away your anger. Let the purple water take you to a safe place where you feel you can unload this anger. Breathe in the oils and let the healing begin.

4. Afterward, unplug your bath and see all that anger go down the drain. Pat yourself dry to keep the bath's wonderful calming energy within you.

For Happiness

This is one of the most fun baths I have ever taken. When I take this bath, I'm happy for the next few days. Let's get started!

1. Set a large bowl in the kitchen. Slice three oranges into thin rings, making sure to use undamaged produce. Add them to the large bowl. Do the same with three limes and three lemons.

Also add fresh lavender flowers, the petals of a few white carnations, and the petals of two white roses. Next, add some green grapes, a few pieces of pineapple (preferably fresh), and a bunch of fresh mint leaves. Mix it all together, but mix gently so you don't damage the flowers.

2. Take the bowl into the bathroom and start filling the tub. Turn on soft, relaxing music, then light as many multicolored candles as you'd like. I recommend using multicolored candles to wake up the body's chakras, but you can use plain candles if that's all you have.

3. Pour two cans of coconut milk into the bathwater. Add bergamot and geranium essential oils and a few drops of yellow food coloring. Finally, gently add the bowl's contents to the bath. Are you smiling yet?

4. Once you are in the bathwater, make yourself a part of this experience by letting every ingredient brush against your body. I even recommend rubbing your skin with the ingredients. Stay in the water as long as you'd like, continuing to visualize the happiness you need in your life. You'll know you're

finished when your mood has lifted and you are smiling and happy.

5. When you get out of the bath, pat dry. Pick the ingredients out of the bath and wring them out with your hands, then place them inside a brown paper bag. Take the paper bag to a place that makes you happy and empty the contents. Redo this spell when your happiness starts to dwindle.

15
Colors in Things We Take for Granted

Everything has a color, whether it's a material, mineral, or animal, though some colors are more noticeable than others. We make choices based on color when we purchase things like clothes or decorations, though we may not even be aware we are doing it! Color dominates the physical realm, but we tend to only work with it in the magical one. In this chapter, I'm going to share how something as irrelevant as a pen can tap into magical properties.

Think of all the items you use on a regular basis. I'm guessing that never in your wildest dreams would you have associated them with magic or considered using them to influence an outcome, but there is a spiritual and magical force behind everything we touch, hold, and keep nearby.

Anything that has a color has a magical property, and it can be used to cause an effect, no matter how insignificant you may think the item is. Everything is programmable because it all comes from Mother Nature. Even if the item in question has been processed or dyed, it is still a part of nature, which means its magic cannot easily be dismissed. A tube of red lipstick can be used for makeup or courage. A safety pin can be used to fasten something but can also provide protection when needed. This chapter will share other ways to invite in everyday magic.

Balloons

Balloons come in all sorts of colors. These are perfect for getting rid of bottled-up emotions, especially anger. I like to use blue balloons. Blow up a balloon until it is almost full. With every breath of air you send into the balloon, send what you want to let go of inside as well. Once you get the balloon to the desired size, pop it with a pin.

Umbrellas

Umbrellas protect us from rain, snow, or sun. Naturally, umbrellas are a great protection tool. Place a closed black umbrella behind your front door. This represents readiness for whatever negative energy comes to the front door. You could also place a colored umbrella behind the door. Try:

- Blue to keep the peace in the home
- Pink to protect love
- Green to protect finances
- Yellow to keep children interested in learning
- Purple for spiritual energy

Tea Towels

I have white and brown tea towels in my kitchen to keep everything in order. These are very grounding colors. White and brown tea towels will also encourage you to experiment with new recipes you've never dared to make before.

Clothes

Every morning, without failure, I do the ritual in front of my wardrobe, the "what to wear" ritual. Some people are quick and unwavering in their choice, whereas others try on three or four outfits before they decide on one. What we wear is an indication of our style and mood, and the wrong outfit or color can make or break our day. Here is a quick color guide that will help you decide when to wear the following colors.

Black: Wear the color black when you have something pressing to communicate at work or in your personal life, when you need to warn someone of an unpleasant outcome, or when you need protection.

Blue: Wear dark blue during a job interview for a positive outcome. Wear light blue when you need people to listen to your ideas, thoughts, or emotions, and when you are having difficulties being understood.

Yellow: This is the perfect color to wear while studying, attending a class, or trying to retain information. It's also great to wear yellow on days you'll be out in the sun. And, of course, wear yellow for happiness.

Red: Wear red when you need to attract someone, for power, and for courage.

White: Wear white when health problems occur, while doing spiritual workings, while meditating, or when out with nature. If you are having problems choosing an outfit, choose something white, as you can never go wrong on a spiritual level.

Orange: This color boosts communication, so it is great to wear in meetings or at parties. It's a very joyful color; unexpected blessings could come into your life just by letting orange in for the day.

Purple: If you know you are going to have a stressful day, wear purple. It will calm you and soothe some of your anxiety. You can also wear purple for clearer communication with the spiritual realm. I recommend wearing purple when trying to get in touch with your guides.

Pink: What a great color to wear when feeling low! Wear pink when you go to gatherings that may lead to new friendships or romantic love.

Green: Green is the color of growth in every aspect. Wear green when growth is needed for the day, whether it is emotional, romantic, or financial growth you need.

Paint Colors

There are so many options to choose from when painting the inside and outside of your home. This is ultimately up to you and your personal preferences, of course, but I wanted to share some painting recommendations if you want more color magic in your life. (If you cannot paint the walls where you live, decorate the rooms with that color instead.)

- Paint children's rooms pastel green or light yellow to infuse learning and happiness.
- Paint the home office pastel green for growth and development.
- Incorporate red in the master bedroom for hearty lovemaking. Paint at least one wall red if you can. Otherwise, decorate the master bedroom with a red item that stands out, such as a large red vase, a red picture frame, or red bed linens.
- Have a blue kettle in the kitchen—even if it's just for decoration—for harmony, balance, and, of course, prosperity.

- Paint the family room orange. Decorate with something orange that stands out, like a painting with several different shades of orange, to maintain harmony and spiritual balance.

Stationery

Putting words to paper is very powerful—even more so when used in your magical workings. Stationary has endless magical purposes, so I recommend keeping your home or office well stocked with supplies. Set aside special pens, ink, paper, and envelopes that will only be used for magical purposes.

Use a black pen when writing on colored paper, and if you want to use colored ink, make sure to use white paper so you can see what you are writing. On your stationary, write down what you want (or don't want). Make sure to write as if your wish has already been granted or is in progress. Never write "if"—write "when."

Once finished, you can roll up the paper to keep the energy, or you can burn the paper. You can scatter the ashes, bury them, or ask the wind to take them where you want them. There is no right or wrong way to go about this.

Here are a few stationary combinations for magical use.

Love Note: Pink paper and black pen

Money Needs: Green paper and black pen

Letting Go: White paper and purple pen

Healing a Relationship: Blue paper and black pen

For Health: Blue paper and black pen

Repelling Evil: Black paper and a white marker (bury this one and keep it underground, where it should be)

Positivity: White paper and orange pen

Nail Polish

A while back, most people painted their nails one of three or four colors. These were different shades of reds, pinks, and corals. Nowadays, nail polish is fun, bright, and varied; there is a color for everyone. You can even use nail stickers or nail art to celebrate birthdays and festivities such as Christmas. Why not incorporate nail polish into your magical workings? Paint your nails according to your needs.

Red: Courage

Orange: Self-expression

Yellow: Intuition

Green: Growth and financial development

Blue: Protection and peace

Purple: Meditation and healing

White: Purity and understanding

Black: Protection

Pink: Love and self-love

Brown: Stability

Handkerchief

You can use a handkerchief to wipe your nose or dry your tears. These little, square cloths are making a comeback! Even if you don't use handkerchiefs, keep a white hanky in your pocket or handbag to absorb emotional upsets.

Tableware

It would be expensive to constantly change your tableware, but you can easily swap out other items without too much cost, such as table-cloths, napkins, and placemats. I change my table linens depending on the occasion. For a peaceful family dinner, use blue items. Use red and orange table linens for a party, yellow for a workshop, and pink and white for a romantic dinner. As you set down every item, visualize a harmonious meal, party, or gathering in your home.

Fruits

Just like herbs, all fruits have a special magical property, but most of us never think to use them as magical ingredients. When putting away fruit or placing it in a bowl, remember to visualize how that specific fruit can benefit you and your home. Here is a list of some common fruits and their attributes.

Green (Grapes): Attracts money to the home

Orange (Oranges): Increases laughter and happiness

Red (Strawberries): Boosts love and luck

Red (Apples): Brings good luck, especially if displayed in the dining room

Yellow (Bananas): Blesses the home with prosperity

Underwear

The color of your underwear can be a beacon for finding love in your life. I recommend pink if you are looking, and red if you need passion in your life.

My dad taught me this old remedy to find love: on the back of your underwear, on top of the elastic, stitch a small red bow facing outward. This will attract lovers to you.

Workspace

Most of us have work responsibilities that we do so many times they become routine, almost ritualistic. Your workspace is sacred, just like your sacred space at home. Protecting your workspace is just as important as protecting your home, especially considering how many hours a week are spent at work.

To protect yourself from unnecessary stress and negative interactions at work, decorate your workspace with black and red. Program a tiger's eye crystal to protect you and then place it on your desk. Try to put it somewhere people will not touch it; if they do, cleanse the crystal and reprogram it. Set or hang a mirror in your workspace to reflect others' negative energy.

Magical School

Specific colors encourage children to concentrate on their school-work. Make yellow, orange, and green their school colors to retain lessons learned. You could dress children in these colors or substitute clothing with pens, pencils, book covers, and pencil cases. I also recommend stashing a citrine crystal somewhere in their school bag.

Traffic Lights

There are three colors on a traffic light: red, yellow, and green. I think sitting at a red light is one of the most boring parts of driving. Why not take a moment and use the lights for a mini visualization instead?

While waiting for the lights to change, think about a situation where courage is needed, or visualize something you are passionate about coming to fruition. Then, when the light turns green, see this as a message from the Universe that your concerns have been heard.

Towels

When we take a shower or bath, we are not only cleaning our physical body, but also our emotional one. Remember, water is cleansing: it removes real dirt *and* spiritual dirt. I do my best crying in the shower. After a good shower cry, I always feel light and refreshed. My whole mood changes. Once out, I pat myself dry with a fluffy white towel to keep these wonderful energies in my physical and emotional bodies.

If you've had a rough day at work, take a shower and pat dry with a blue towel to find peace within. A red towel after a shower or bath seals the energy for a passionate night. I recommend yellow towels for students of any age, green towels for growth and emotional healing, pink towels for self-love, and black towels to protect yourself from negative energy.

Vases

A vase holds the beauty of nature within it. Vases are usually made out of clear glass, but you can find them in all sorts of different colors, shapes, sizes, and designs. Most people have vases at home that they only bring out when there are fresh flowers to display, but if you

don't have any flowers, you can still use your vase! Vases can magically bring in certain energies. A blue vase in the home helps maintain open conversation. Green vases keep money flowing in, yellow invites new experiences into the home, purple calls in peace and tranquility, red promotes courage, and orange brings happiness.

In Closing

There is nothing more rewarding than seeing your dreams and desires manifest because of your magical workings.

Never get discouraged: magic is not a twenty-four manifestation. It takes time and patience, but rest assured it will work—though sometimes not the way you thought it would. Magic gifts you with options and opportunities you never thought possible. It changes your life, and always for the best.

Have fun, harm none, and enjoy seeing your deepest wishes come true with color magic.

Blessings,
Ileana

Appendix
Quick Color Guide

Below is a quick color guide for you to use. This is a basic guide, so if you can't find what you need here, there are plenty of colors you can work with that are not on this list. You could also try blending a few colors; pay attention to the effects. Make notes so you know what color blends work well for you. There is no right or wrong way to blend colors. Experimenting is how we learn!

Black: Protection, balancing negative energy (best used with white), use cautiously to do no harm

Blue: Peace, protection, healing, communication, relaxation, stress reduction

Brown: Healing emotions, communication, self-awareness, intellect, reliability

Green: Money, growth (great for children's growth and development), seeking forgiveness, spiritual growth

Gold: Communication with higher realms of existence, strengthening the mind and intuition

Lavender: Peace, harmony, courage, soothing chronic conditions, peace of mind and spirit, anxiety reduction, settling past emotional upsets

Lilac: Peace, learning lessons, bravery

Orange: Intuition, happiness, encouragement, wisdom, learning new skills, expressing emotions

Pink: Love, understanding, self-love, calm, forgiveness

Red: Courage, emotional strength, leadership, passion, lust, attraction

Silver: Feminine energy, meditation, communication with the Goddess, reflection, manifestation of dreams, enhancement, healing (adults and children)

Violet: Visions of the future, imagination, meditation, compassion, psychic work

White: Purity, meditation, healing; can be a substitution for any color on the spectrum

Yellow: Happiness, learning and understanding, confidence, assurance, emotional stability, warmth

A Rainbow Spell for Joy

I leave you with this simple way to make someone happy: Get a glass bowl and fill it with thousands of nonpareils sprinkles. Write down the name of the person that needs a bit of happiness in their lives, then set this scrap of paper deep in the bowl. They will be surrounded by joy.

To Write to the Author

If you wish to contact the author or would like more information about this book, please write to the author in care of Llewellyn Worldwide Ltd. and we will forward your request. Both the author and publisher appreciate hearing from you and learning of your enjoyment of this book and how it has helped you. Llewellyn Worldwide Ltd. cannot guarantee that every letter written to the author can be answered, but all will be forwarded. Please write to:

Ileana Abrev
% Llewellyn Worldwide
2143 Wooddale Drive
Woodbury, MN 55125-2989

Please enclose a self-addressed stamped envelope for reply,
or $1.00 to cover costs. If outside the U.S.A., enclose
an international postal reply coupon.

Many of Llewellyn's authors have websites with additional information and resources. For more information, please visit our website at http://www.llewellyn.com.